Rail

New Holland
and the
Humber Ferries

by
A.J. Ludlam

THE OAKWOOD PRESS

© Oakwood Press & A.J. Ludlam 1996

British Library Cataloguing in Publication Data
A Record for this book is available from the British Library
ISBN 0 85361 494 6

Typeset by Oakwood Graphics.
Repro by Ford Graphics, Ringwood, Hants.
Printed by The Witney Press, Witney, Oxon.

Dedication

For John Addison, Northumbrian Pipe Maker and Railway Enthusiast

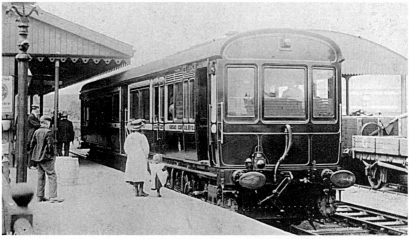

A Great Central Railway motor train stands in Barton station in 1911.
David Lee Collection

Front cover: The fireman moves the coal forward on class 'D10' 4-4-0 No. 5429 *Prince Henry*, prior to working the 2.30 pm train to Lincoln on 10th May, 1946. No. 5429 was named *Sir Alexander Henderson* until 1917, when it became *Sir Douglas Haig* for about three years.   *H.C. Casserley*

Title page: This view of New Holland pier shows off the signalling to good advantage. A ferry waits at the pontoon on 10th May, 1946.   *H.C. Casserley*

Published by
The Oakwood Press
P.O. Box 122, Headington, Oxford, OX3 8LU.

Contents

MS&LR 0-4-2 No. 269 enters Thornton Abbey station with a Cleethorpes bound train. Notice the elegant lamp standards and the busy siding behind the down platform.
Author's Collection

A view of a busy New Holland Dock with Humber keels in evidence, *c.* 1908.
Grimsby Public Library

A comprehensive view of New Holland Pier and Dock. The Humber ferry *Wingfield Castle* is berthed alongside the pontoon. *Author's Collection*

Introduction

The estuary of the River Humber, with its strong tidal currents and constantly shifting sandbanks, is one of the great natural barriers of the United Kingdom. Part of the boundary between the counties of Yorkshire and Lincolnshire, it is formed by the junctions of the rivers Ouse and Trent, and empties into the North Sea, south of Spurn Head.

In AD 47 the Roman 9th Legion was established at Lincoln, from where they built Ermine Street, the road ending on rising ground on the south bank of the Humber, half a mile east of the village of Wintringham. It was between here and Petvaria (Brough) on the north bank that the first regular river crossings were made. In later years Petvaria became the site of the *Transitus Marimus* - 'very great ferry'.

Over the centuries the number of ferries and crossing places increased and, in 1803, Thomas Dent operated the first ferry between New Holland and Hull, using an open boat. It was, however, Joseph Brown of Barton, who, with his friends, established the first regular ferry service between New Holland and Hull. By 1832 the *Magna Charta* was providing three round trips a day, and by 1846 70,000 travellers were using the service.

It was, then, no surprise that the emergent railway companies should look to control the crossing of the Humber and with it access to Hull in particular. The New Holland to Hull ferry was purchased by the Great Grimsby & Sheffield Junction Railway, in 1845, the company later becoming part of the Manchester, Sheffield & Lincolnshire Railway (MS&LR), and, in 1897, the Great Central Railway. The ferry service continued under the auspices of the LNER and British Railways, its demise coinciding with the opening of the Humber Bridge in June 1981.

The last three paddle steamers all survived. The *Tattershall Castle* became a restaurant, moored near Westminster Bridge, in London. The *Wingfield Castle*, went firstly to Brighton and later to Hartlepool. For a time the *Lincoln Castle* was beached near Hessle under the shadow of the Humber Bridge. She was moved from this rather undignified position in May 1987, and is now berthed alongside the National Fishing Heritage Centre, in the Alexandra Dock, Grimsby, serving as a pub and restaurant.

This is the story of the metamorphosis of a bleak, windswept and thinly populated area of North Lincolnshire, from fen and farmland into an important railway colony, which was, for a time in the mid-1800s, the eastern terminus of the MS&LR.

An everyday sight at one time, as workers left the ferry at New Holland.   *C.T. Goode*

5

An engraving published in about 1843 of the New Holland ferry.   *Authors Collection*

An engraving featured in the *Illustrated London News* of 15th April, 1848, showing the pier at New Holland and the ferry. The illustration accompanied an article describing the opening of the East Lincolnshire Railway between Louth and Grimsby and onwards via the MS&LR to New Holland and Hull.

Chapter One

New Holland

In 1316 King Edward II granted a charter to the Warden and Burgesses of Hull to operate a ferry between Hull and Lincolnshire. The carriage of pedestrians was to cost a halfpenny each, equestrians one penny, a cart with a pair of horses, twopence and bigger items at a proportional rate. The landing on the Lincolnshire side was to be at Barton. The Barton and Hull ferry was instituted by a grant made at Lincoln in the Wardenship of Robert de Sandal in 1316.

In 1688 the scale of charges for the Barton and Hull ferry was signed by the Mayor of Hull, B.B. Thompson and G. Uppleby, lessee of the Barton ferry:

> Stranger from Barton to Hull, in Hull boats, pays sixpence, fourpence being returned to the Barton Ferryman; Inhabitants of Hull pay nothing to the Barton Ferryman; Freemen of Hull pay sixpence for a man and a horse in the Hull boat, and the inhabitants (of Hull) pay eightpence. If a stranger be carried from Barton to Hull in the Hull boat, he pays one shilling, the whole of which goes to the Barton Ferryman. If an inhabitant or freeman [presumably of Hull] goes in the Hoy,* he pays fourpence, if in the horseboat without a horse, twopence.
>
> If a stranger and his horse is carried from Barton to Hull, he pays fourpence, a penny of which is paid to the Barton Ferryman, but if he goes from Hull to Barton in the Hoy, he pays fourpence, all of which is kept by the Hull Ferryman.

In 1759 J. Coote observed,

> Barton is a mean straggling town in Yarborough Wapentake, and Lindsey Division, in the north of Lincolnshire. It is situated on the south shore of the Humber; over which at this place, a sorry and dangerous passage to Hull in an open ferry boat, in which sometimes fifteen horses, ten or twelve cows, intermingle with seventeen or eighteen passengers and are tossed about four hours or more on the Humber before they can get to the harbour at Hull.

The Hull Guide of 1806, described the service as operated by 'not less than four large boats of 45 ton burthen and several smaller ones which will take fifteen to twenty-five persons each'. As many as 300 people sometimes crossed the Humber by the Hoy at this time, particularly on Sunday afternoons.

Besides the passenger boats there were also horse boats, capable of carrying four gentlemen's four-wheeled carriages, an equal number of gigs and up to 50 horses on each tide. Boats made the passage in 40 to 50 minutes, seldom longer than two hours and the average did not exceed one hour 20 minutes. The smaller boats were often hired by people who had missed the Hoy.

> The principal obstruction which the ferry is at any time subject to is when the Hull harbour is crowded with boats. It cannot reach the proper landing stage and passengers have to cross several vessels or use small boats to make a landing. This frequently happens when large fleets are coming or going out. It will be removed when the bason [sic] is completed by the Corporation for the sole use of the ferry and the market boats.

---

* A small sloop rigged vessel engaged in light traffic such as passengers and goods.

In the early 1800s passengers and goods were transported across the Humber from a number of points along the Lincolnshire coast. Market boats made regular journeys to Hull from small creeks and havens such as Stallingborough, Goxhill, Barrow and Wintringham. Some boats made the journey twice a week to catch the Tuesday and Fridays markets in Hull, quite a few sailed once a week and some once a fortnight. There were so many at this time that it was thought not a single village along the banks of the Humber was without its own market boat.

The owners of the ancient ferries actively discouraged more frequent trips by the market boats, sometimes resorting to legal action to try to restrict competition.

The shortest crossing of the Humber lay between Wintringham Haven and Brough, the oldest from Barton to Hessle (the eventual course of the Humber Bridge), but their popularity was superseded in the early 1800s by the Barton-Hull route. Although this was longer it had the important advantage of coach connections at each side of the river.

The Humber ferries depended on the tides. At new or full moon, they would sail at 3 o'clock on the first day, 4 o'clock on the second day, 5 o'clock on the third and so on for a six day duration. At the quarter days they would sail at 9 o'clock, 10, 11, 12 and so on until the sixth day. If the wind was from the west or south-west, the boats would sail on the half hour before the time mentioned. Boats left Barton for Hull two hours after their arrival time at Barton.

The ferry service between New Holland and Hull had very humble and decidedly dubious beginnings. Thomas Dent occupied land belonging to the churchwardens of Barrow-on-Humber, in the recently enclosed Oxmarsh of that parish. This was close to a main drain outlet into the Humber. It was here that soon after 1803 Dent built a house and a large shed, the creek taking Dent's name because of the association.

Dent operated a ferry between here and Hull, which consisted of a small boat worked by himself and an assistant. There appears to be little doubt that Dent's ferry was merely a facade behind which operated a much more lucrative activity in smuggled goods. The *Lincoln, Rutland and Stamford Mercury* described Dent's undertaking thus,

This primitive state of things lasted for some time, when the convenience of landing afforded by the creek, the isolated position of the spot, the paucity of inhabitants, with other collateral advantages, pointed it out as an eligible place for the debarkation of smuggled goods, but more especially of Holland's gin, and, it was notoriously used as such, hence it obtained the name New Holland.

Thomas Dent's 'ferry' had little effect on the established services and would most likely have faded into obscurity had it not been for the appearance of Joseph Brown, of Barton. Brown and some influential friends bought some land near Oxmarsh Creek, in Barrow, and formed a company known as the New Holland Proprietors. Their intention was to develop a river crossing at that point. In 1825 they purchased a small boat and the following year built the 'Yarborough Arms' for the convenience of their customers; this was the first, and, for many years, the only public building in New Holland. There appears to be some difference of opinion about the regularity of the new ferry service, some claimed that from 1828 onwards a daily service by sailing boat operated, other opinion claimed the company ran only 'an occasional passage to Hull'. Brown's original intention of running a steam ferry with coach connections, in direct competition with the Barton ferry, was certainly postponed until the road to New Holland had been improved.

At the beginning of the 1800s, because of steam navigation, the importance of the Barton to Hull ferry had increased, the *Royal Charter* making four trips a day, each way, as against previous sailings of one or two a day, according to the tide. This resulted in an increase in stage coach traffic to Barton and a considerable rise in coach and ferry fares. A reform agitator, James Acland, maintained that Hull Corporation could not legally charge more than a halfpenny, as stipulated by the charter granted by King Edward II five centuries before. When the Corporation rejected Acland's assertions he declared he would run a ferry boat in opposition to the official steamer.

Because of Acland's extremely limited means he was only able to hire a smaller, inferior boat from Messrs Furley & Company of Gainsborough; originally named *Victory*, she was renamed *Public Opinion* by Acland.

Acland's opposition was launched in September 1831, with crowds in attendance to witness the events at Hull and Barton. Although the crossings began at a halfpenny rate they soon increased to fourpence. Even so this was still considerably cheaper than the official ferry, and, as a result, Acland gained most of the traffic, resulting in losses by the Corporation steamer. An injunction to try and curb Acland's activities was refused by the courts. What resorting to the law failed to achieve was, in fact, accomplished by circumstances. In December Acland announced that he had spent £200 and incurred a further £150 in liabilities during the period of his opposition. As a result he had decided to suspend services over the winter period, when traffic declined considerably. The old *Public Opinion* was in need of costly repairs and returned to Gainsborough.

A proposal to persuade the Humber Packet Company to build a new steamer for the start of the Opposition trade on 1st May, 1832 was not sufficiently supported and opposition to the official service ceased briefly.

The New Holland scheme, proposed by Joseph Brown in 1825, had Acland's support and no doubt benefited from his campaign against the fares charged on the Barton-Hull service. The New Holland Proprietors increased their capital by involving more shareholders and revived their earlier plans for the purchase of a steamer and improved road access to New Holland.

By the autumn of 1832 the *Magna Charta* was providing a service of three round trips a day between New Holland and Hull, with an extra trip on Hull market days. Not long afterwards a daily 'hoss', or horse boat, was introduced for the carriage of livestock.

A major problem at New Holland was the lack of a suitable landing facility. At low water great areas of mud flats are exposed. It was decided that a jetty would alleviate the problem.

The approach road to New Holland was improved, allowing regular coaching and mail services to connect with the ferry. Coaches running from New Holland at this time included the *Pelham*, to Boston, the *Magna Charta*, to Nottingham, via Lincoln, and the *Age*, which at first connected with Boston but was later directed to Lincoln.

The 'Yarborough Arms' was enlarged, allowing more accommodation for travellers and providing a tea garden, skittle ground and bowling green. One or two more buildings appeared, including a house built for the ferry superintendent.

The rapid expansion of railways throughout the country resulted in cut-throat competition between rival coach companies, for what was a shrinking market. In 1836 the London Mail was transferred from Barton to New Holland. This, allied to the shorter crossing between New Holland and Hull, conspired to weaken further the Barton ferry, which had never fully recovered from its brush with Joseph Acland's opposition service.

By 1846 it was estimated that 70,000 people were passing through New Holland. In 1848 the settlement comprised very few buildings, with the population almost exclusively employed by the ferry company or connecting coach services. Because of the well synchronised ferry and coach services, travellers tended not to stay overnight at the 'Yarborough Arms', at best they would partake of a meal. During the summer months the steamers would bring day-trippers (a new phenomena which would be offered even greater opportunities by the emergent railway companies) from Hull, Gainsborough and Selby to visit the inn's pleasure gardens and enjoy a trip to Spurn Point at the mouth of the Humber.

In 1842 there were more than 25 paddle steamers working on the Humber from Hull to Grimsby, New Holland, Gainsborough, Goole, Selby, Thorne, York and other places.

MS&LR Paddle Steamer *Manchester c.* 1849.   *Illustrated London News*

Chapter Two

Birth of the Manchester, Sheffield & Lincolnshire Railway and Some Duplicitous Dealing

The companies which the Act of Amalgamation of 27th July, 1846 brought together to form the Manchester, Sheffield & Lincolnshire Railway were the Sheffield, Ashton-under-Lyne and Manchester Railway (SA&M), which at that time was operational; the Great Grimsby and Sheffield Junction Railway (GG&SJ) and the Sheffield and Lincolnshire Junction Railway (S&LJ), both about to be constructed; and the Grimsby Docks Company (GDC), the oldest of the four progenitors and the company largely responsible for the early development of the commercial docks in Grimsby. The Grimsby Docks Act of 8th August, 1845 had dissolved the GDC's predecessor, the Grimsby Haven Company, vesting its interests in the new company. The GDC and the GG&SJ shared several Directors, Lord Worsley, Richard Thorold, Michael Ellison, George Heneage and James Wall.

At a well attended public meeting, which launched the GG&SJ, held at the Red Lion Hotel, in Caistor, on 28th October, 1844, it was resolved to construct a railway from Grimsby to Gainsborough. A further meeting at the Town Hall in Grimsby, on 6th November, considered three possible routes suggested by John Fowler, the Engineer. Firstly via Caistor (34¾ miles, summit level 232 feet); secondly, Brigg (36½ miles, summit level 115 feet); and third, via Market Rasen (37¼ miles, summit level 237 feet). The assembly approved the route via Brigg, with a resolution to build a branch from there to Market Rasen. Support was also expressed for the S&LJ, which would link the GG&SJ and the SA&M, providing a continuous rail link between Grimsby and Manchester.

By the end of 1844 the GG&SJ had achieved an understanding with the Grimsby Haven Company which prepared the way for the formation of the Grimsby Docks Company. The GDC would seek powers in the 1845 Session of Parliament, to extend the docks, at the same time the GG&SJ would try to secure its Act of Incorporation. By May 1845 the estimates for its construction were ready.

Main Line	£389,929
Market Rasen branch	£30,385
New Holland branch	£27,730

These prices were exclusive of rails, chairs and the land and stations.

In 1844 the provisional committee of the GG&SJ discovered that one of the lines under the control of George Hudson had made a bid for the New Holland ferry. Their reaction was swift, contact with the New Holland Proprietors established an asking price of £11,000. The package included the old Barrow ferry rights, as well as the following:

New Holland
Yarborough Arms and Gardens
Stabling, Coach Houses and Granaries
Foldyard, Piggeries and 7 acre Field
Foreshore, Jetty, Wharf and Land
Warehouse and Coalyard.

Barrow Old Ferry
Public House and Warehouse
Granary and Two Acre Field

The provisional committee made a bid of £10,000 subject to the Required Act of Parliament being granted. The ferry owners rejected the offer, maintaining that their price was a fair one and they would accept no conditions.

With the Hudson threat adding some urgency to the proceedings, the provisional committee asked Robert Smith, of Ancaster, to carry out an immediate survey of the ferry properties. His report of 1st January, 1845 commended the deal and stated that he expected the value of the property to increase whether or not the GG&SJ secured its Act of Parliament. The net annual revenue was £420 and the full cost of purchase £11,800. Smith further emphasised his assessment by indicating an interest in investing in the project himself.

The provisional committee decided to

. . . consider the propriety of treating and agreeing, and if so determined, to agree with the owners of certain Ferries, called, Barrow Ferry, New Holland Ferry and Goxhill Ferry, situate near the aforesaid (proposed) Railway, for the purchase of such Ferries, or any of them, and the landings, land, buildings and appurtenances belonging thereto, or any part or parts of such land or buildings.

The deliberations did not take long and the provisional committee decided to go ahead and purchase the ferries. The guarantors were Messrs Woodcroft, Dobson, Smith, Ellison, Ward, Dr Holland, Messrs Humfrey, Fowler, Randall, Wall and Howe, the surveyor Robert Smith, Messrs Hinde and Gainford the GG&SJ solicitors, plus two outsiders, G. Smith and J. Hett.

A meeting was held with the ferry owners on 10th January, 1845, at which the provisional committee repeated its offer of £10,000. The New Holland Proprietors agreed to the price and the deal was completed. Eight days later the provisional committee agreed to purchase the Goxhill ferry for £300. The following statement was contained in a GG&SJ advertisement which appeared in the *Sheffield & Rotherham Independent*, on 18th January,

The directors have also to announce that they have, on their own responsibility, purchased from the proprietors the whole of their valuable property and privileges in the ferries from New Holland and Barrow to Hull, with land and buildings at both landing places, deeming it most important to the success of the undertaking that the property at once be secured by them, and essential to the future working of the Railway that the arrangements for the Ferry should be under their control.

The implication appeared to be that the provisional committee had made the purchase on behalf of the GG&SJ, to be held in trust until the Act of Parliament was obtained. By the end of January, however, the Secretary of the provisional committee, Lt Col J.H. Humfrey, was told to make no reference of the purchase of the Humber ferries in the company records. Solicitor Hinde, who had himself put £500 towards the purchase, was advised that, 'after 1st January, 1845 you must be taken as acting for the parties in their private capacity and not as the provisional committee of the GG&SJ Company'. The scheme was now a private speculation involving 14 members of the provisional committee. Humfrey, who had originally agreed to become a shareholder but had backed out, was invited to take up shares. He, along with William Smith of the solicitors and Dr de Bartolome, refused.

The GG&SJ received Royal Assent on 30th June, having bought off the threat of the rival Hull & Gainsborough project by means of £6,000 paid to its promoters. The first shareholders' meeting took place on 27th August. At the meeting it was agreed that the New Holland ferry should be purchased by the company; negotiations as to the purchase price, because of the 'consequence of some Directors having a personal interest in the ferries', was entrusted to John Rodgers, William Smith, Thomas Newmarsh and Mark Favell.

The ferry owners nominated Ellison, Woodcroft and Howe to meet the company representatives and offer the undertaking for sale at a price of £21,000, 'the Railway Company paying all expenses, legal and otherwise, relative to its purchase by its present owners and to the sale of the said Ferries to the Railway Company'.

A remarkable piece of chicanery was completed when the Company agreed to the price and finalised the deal when three members of the Board, who were not also owners of the ferries, instructed one of their number, Lord Worsley, to write to the solicitors, (who were acting for both parties), as follows, 'I beg to inform you that I have consulted Mr James Dixon and Mr Thomas James Dixon as to the purchase of the Ferries across the Humber, and they both concur with me in recommending the purchase by the company at the price asked for by the gentlemen who possessed themselves of the Ferries at a considerable risk'.

The Board of the GG&SJ approved the price on the same day and the purchase was ratified at a meeting of Directors, eight of whom were also numbered amongst the 14 owners of the ferries, at a meeting at Normanton on 8th October. In less than nine months the so-called trustees for the company had made a clear profit of £11,000 with little risk to themselves.

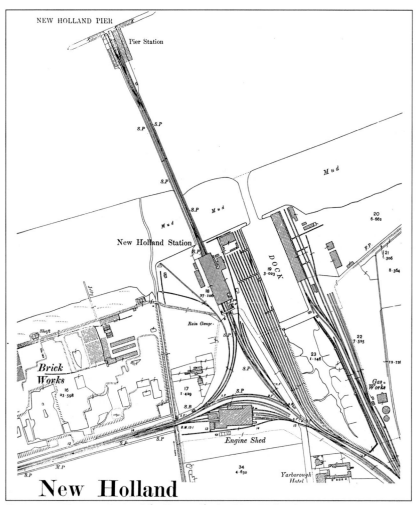

New Holland

Pier station, Town station and the Engine Shed at New Holland.

Reproduced from the 25", 1908 Ordnance Survey Map

TABLE 1

THE INDUSTRIAL AND OCCUPATIONAL STRUCTURE OF
NEW HOLLAND IN 1851

(Males 16 years of age and over)

Employed on the railways (drivers, firemen, guards, porters, etc.)	Employed on the river and on the docks (watermen, coastguards, dock labourers, etc.)	Employed in agriculture (farmers and agricultural labourers)	Employed in brickmaking	Others (masons, bricklayers, butchers, shopkeepers, etc.)
75	24	9	5	29

Source: Enumeration returns 1851, parish of Barrow upon Humber.
N.B. The totals must be regarded as approximate. Doubtful cases are
included in the category "Others", and it is likely that this group is rather
larger than it was in reality.

Chapter Three

New Holland, Railway Colony

The GG&SJ decided to establish New Holland as the terminal of a branch from its line between Grimsby and Gainsborough. This plan was progressed by the new company, when the GG&SJ was amalgamated, with others, to become the MS&LR. The Grimsby to Gainsborough line was constructed by John Stephenson & Co. and opened in three sections, Grimsby to Brocklesby on 1st March, 1848; Brocklesby to Brigg in November 1848 and Brigg to Gainsborough on 2nd April, 1849. The first section was part of the New Holland line, which opened on the same day and in conjunction with the East Lincolnshire line, between Grimsby and Louth. This line was leased to the Great Northern Railway, who shared the provision of trains between Louth and New Holland with the MS&L. At New Holland a connecting ferry service was provided, and expanded, by the purchase of two second-hand iron paddle steamers, the *Queen*, and the *Prince of Wales*, from the Gravesend Steamboat Company.

The *Railway Chronicle* reported the passage of the MS&L Directors to New Holland from Hull in one of the newly purchased boats, on 29th February, 1848.

The passage was effected in a quarter of an hour. At New Holland we first touched upon the works. A pier 1,500 feet in length extends into the water, and will not only enable passengers to embark and disembark at all times of the tide, but forms a continuation of the station and the platform. It will be covered and lighted with gas and the rails of the New Holland line will be continued to the extremity, so that passengers to and from Hull will have to make but a step between the pier and the steamboats.

A dock of 3 acres, bounded by another pier, also provided with double lines of rails, is in a forward state, for the exclusive accommodation of merchandise and cattle. The Directors and their friends, after examining the station, proceeded to the 'Yarborough Arms' for breakfast. This inn and a small ferry house were, until lately, the only buildings to be seen at New Holland, where, for miles around, the country stretches out in all the flat luxuriance of a Flemish landscape. At 10.00 am the party took their places in a train of five carriages, for Grimsby, a distance of 16 miles. In the distance there are five intermediate stations. About six miles from New Holland we reached a spot where a junction will be formed with the line from Gainsborough and Sheffield, through Glanford Brigg. Passing into the Brocklesby domains, which the line intersects for nearly eight miles, we came to Ulceby, where the New Holland Branch, on which we had been travelling, joins the main line by forming one side of a triangle. From New Holland, until we reached Grimsby, the route lies through country presenting no great engineering difficulties, no heavy embankments or deep cuttings, the chief works being bridges and culverts for the accommodation of the many drains intersected. We arrived at Grimsby at about 10.45 am and were met on the platform by the Mayor and corporation of that ancient borough, and a party of Directors of the East Lincolnshire. The Grimsby Station is intended to be used jointly by the two companies, and so is situated that it may easily be extended at either extremity. After some delay, at about 2.00 pm, we proceeded to Louth, on the line of the East Lincolnshire. The distance from Grimsby to Louth is 14 miles of nearly the most direct and level line in England. The substantial but economical manner in which it has been executed reflects the greatest credit on the engineer. After a short stay at Louth we returned through Grimsby for dinner.

It must be observed that the East Lincolnshire line has been leased to the Great Northern. So far these two railways only afford local accommodation for the traffic passing between Hull, New Holland, Grimsby and the town of Louth; but in the autumn it is expected that the GNR will have opened a complete communication from Louth, through Boston to Peterborough. When this communication is opened, passengers, by the aid of the London North Western and the Eastern Counties, will be able to travel direct from Hull to the Metropolis, saving nearly 40 miles in distance and about 10 shillings in money.

A corresponding journey took place in the opposite direction on the same day, reported in the *Stamford Mercury*:

In about half an hour the whole arrived at Grimsby station (from Louth), and were put in contrast (much to the advantage of the Louth train), with one from New Holland, which was soon on its way to Louth. Half an hour after this we moved on, and passing beneath the newly constructed bridge near Grimsby's church, our vehicle passed Brocklesby park and mansion, the seat of Lord Yarborough. On approaching our destination a slight accident gave the passengers an opportunity of witnessing the dexterity of the train servants owing to some points not being so nicely adjusted as was required, two carriages got off the rails, the passengers had to get out, and with the assistance of a short thick plank and the movement of the engine coinciding, in a few minutes the carriages were helped on the line again and the train connected. As soon as we arrived at New Holland where our appetites were sufficiently whetted by a fresh breeze, which had continuously blown, the company sought a repast, but to many in vain, the host at the inn not being able to supply the demand, and the visitors (including several of the Town Council), luckily falling in with an old jack tar with gingerbread buns on his stall, it was completely eaten up with peculiar relish.

After viewing the port of Hull, which, with as pleasant an aspect invited the passengers over but which the duration of their stay forbade, so too an inspection of the extended jetty, which seemed as if it would stretch across the whole Humber. The whistle of the engine, equally out of tune with the temper of the passengers gave its significant notice and we were once again seated and in a trice we brought up in our return to Grimsby station. Here passengers would have visited their friends but the usual uncertainty as to the time of departure prevented the indulgence. After waiting half-an-hour for the return of the New Holland train from Louth, it arrived and contained the Manchester, Sheffield and Lincolnshire Directors, who retired with those of the East Lincolnshire to the Granby Inn, to settle some matters connected with the interests of both lines . . . At length the time arrived for our ultimate return, we arrived at Louth, where waiting for the company, two new omnibuses of Messrs Willoughby and Michael, we entered the handsome little bus belonging to the latter and in a few minutes found ourselves at the Masons Arms Hotel, where was provided a dinner for the gentry connected with the line and their friends.

During 1849/50, the 1848 agreement between the GNR and the MS&L, allowing each company's trains to run over the others rails, became the victim of more important national wrangling involving the two companies. The London and North Western Railway saw the imminent opening of the GNR's London terminus as a great source of antagonism. The MS&L did an about face and aligned itself with the 'Euston Square Confederacy', (the LNWR, the Midland and the Lancashire and Yorkshire), in their campaign to block the GNR. The outcome was that the former allies were set upon a course of obstruction. The station authorities at Retford refused to supply water to GNR engines, so hampering the through service between Peterborough and Leeds. At Grimsby, blocks were placed on the rails to prevent GNR trains entering the station, thus preventing running through to New Holland.

On at least one occasion when GNR passengers did reach New Holland, they found that the last ferry had been despatched without them, and they were forced to spend the night in the carriages or in the station. A High Court injunction against the MS&LR supported the GNR's rights to run to New Holland but did nothing to halt the obstructionist tactics. Through running to Louth by the MS&LR ceased on 8th July, 1851, and GNR traffic between Grimsby and New Holland finished by 1st December of that year.

The new pier at New Holland was designed by John Fowler, who later designed the Forth Bridge and planned a Humber tunnel to replace the ferries. Constructed of wood, the pier was 32 feet wide and had two lines of rails as well as a carriage way and footpath and extended into the river for 1,375 feet.

The link westwards to Manchester proved beneficial to the New Holland line, it being designated part of the main line for a brief period. The ferry was, for a time, part of the East Coast route to Scotland, running from Bishopgate, in London, via Peterborough to Grimsby and on to New Holland, where a crossing was made to Hull for trains to Selby and connections to York and beyond.

By the end of 1848 the station and pier had been completed at New Holland and work started on the construction of a small dock. Nineteen houses had been built in addition to those built for the workpeople at the station. By 1850 warehouses, cattle sheds and coal wharves were in place and a timber pond was constructed close by the new dock, timber being loaded onto ships that year. The new dock was 600 ft in length and 200 ft wide. Hydraulic machinery was installed on the quayside to facilitate the raising or lowering of trucks to or from the holds of vessels. There were three 2-ton hydraulic cranes along the east side of the dock and a similar 12 ton crane, on the west side. Originally the west side quay accommodated three shutes used for loading salt and later coal, used by the Royal Navy and loaded here for Gibraltar. In 1872 the centre shute was dismantled and replaced by a hydraulic coal hoist, which was itself dismantled in May 1949. The dock was, at one time, served by as many as 10 sidings on the western side and a similar number on the eastern side, serving both the dock and the timber pond. Twelve cast iron sluices supplied with water from behind the harbour were used in scouring the dock and its entrances.

A landing stage, which rose and fell with the tide, was installed at the end of New Holland pier early in December 1849. This made the transfer between rail and river much easier at all stages of the tide. Constructed entirely of wrought iron, except for the wooden platform, it had watertight bulkheads and at the time was the largest of its kind in the country. Manufactured by E.B. Wilson & Co. of Leeds the landing stage cost £17,500, weighed almost 700 tons, was 400 ft long, 52½ ft wide and 8 feet deep. When the hull of the pontoon had been built it was conveyed in sections over the Aire and Calder Navigation, to Goole. Re-assembled it was launched sideways into the River Ouse and taken by six tugs to New Holland, where the work of installation was completed. The two tubular iron bridges which connected the pier to the pontoon were 140 ft long,

10 ft wide and 10 ft deep.

The floating pontoon was destroyed and sunk in a storm in 1869. It was replaced by sloping pier heads. Further damage to the pier station occurred in January, 1895, when it, and the refreshment rooms, were destroyed by fire; rebuilding was completed in 1898.

Things moved very quickly at New Holland. There was talk of the Port of New Holland, the railway certainly hoping to attract a diversity of cargo, and even consideration of the establishment of customs facilities, a proposal that must have made Tommy Dent turn in his grave.

'Besides the company's houses, private individuals are building terraces, which, no sooner erected, than tenants are immediately obtained, so that cottage building here seems to be a profitable speculation'.

Unpublished census papers and railway company records indicate that by 1851 New Holland had a population of 400; 74 of the 80 houses in the village were occupied and seven new dwellings were under construction. The new 'Yarborough Arms' was built for the MS&L by William Kirk, of Lincoln, and completed in 1851, at a cost of £1,825. Most of the population were employed by the railway company or were dependents of railway employees. Whilst some of those would be working on the company's uncompleted installations, the great majority were employed in the operation of the rail and ferry services. At this time the village was known as the 'Railway Colony'.

Several coastguards lived in the village, as well as people employed in the increasingly important brickmaking industry. This had been well established in the area around Barton and Barrow for many years, and no doubt prospered further with the arrival of the railway. After 1861 several new brickyards were established. In the Parish of Barton there were five brickyards employing 102 people in 1861; by 1900, when the industry was at its peak, there were 15 yards, forming an almost continuous strip along the banks of the Humber. In 1896 there were 10 yards in Barrow and New Holland, as well as a further nine scattered along the north Lincolnshire coast from Burton Stather round to Killingholme. Large numbers of bricks were sent to Hull and Grimsby, but the main markets for pantiles and quality facing bricks were London and the expanding industrial towns of west Yorkshire. The success of the industry had been based largely on water transport, each yard having its works close to a riverbank wharf. Clay was dug on the inland side and shipped to local and inland destinations by Humber sloops and keels.

In 1851 New Holland had two butchers, a grocer and a resident schoolmistress, Miss Salmon. A chapel was built during the year, until then the railway company had allowed religious services to take place in the station waiting room. By 1855 the staff at the school had increased to two, the MS&L guaranteeing a salary of £50 per annum to ensure the education of the children of its employees. A library was provided, and, in 1857, a news room and reading room. The MS&L Board deciding that fines imposed on employees located in, and to the east of, Retford, for committing a breach of the company's regulations should become a fund for the New Holland Library. Similar proceeds accrued west of Retford supported the library at Gorton.

The New Holland ferry had, by 1860, become well-established as the principal river crossing. The village of red brick terraces was to change very little in appearance for the remainder of the century.

The MS&L's first offices in Hull were at Walkington's Lodgings, acquired for £850, in January 1849. In August, 7 Nelson Street became the company's booking office for passengers and parcels, the clerk living in the upper floor of the property. The next door premises became company property in May 1854. Goods traffic to and from New Holland was dealt with at Limekiln Creek, where the MS&L station was connected to the North Eastern Railway depot by a horse-operated line, crossing Wellington Street. Between February 1856, and July 1858 the MS&L premises were operated by the NER under an agreement between the two companies.

The GG&SJ and later the MS&L both had powers to establish proper landing facilities at Hull, but these were never acted upon. The result was that at low tide there was insufficient water for steamers to approach the quays and consequently passengers had to embark and land by small boats. This most unsatisfactory situation was rectified when the MS&L General Manager, Edward Watkin, offered the Mayor of Hull an annual contribution of up to £40 towards the cost of landing facilities at Victoria Pier (this was previously known as Corporation Pier).

In 1849 the discovery of George Hudson's 'manipulations' of railway company accounts reverberated through almost all railway companies in the land. Each shareholder began to consider what his own Directors had been, or might have been, up to. There were those for instance, who thought that the initials MS&L stood for 'Money Sunk and Lost'. It was not surprising, therefore, when the shareholders of that company called for an investigation of the company's affairs. Five shareholders were appointed to examine the state of the company's finances, and assess its future prospects. The five concerned, S.R. Healy, J.C. Jack, G. Houndsfield, T. Grieg and L. Simpson, failed to find any evidence of financial mismanagement. No doubt to the intense relief of the Directors involved in the Humber Ferries deal, they presented the Board in a favourable light, their report containing very little not already known by the shareholders.

However, as more of Hudson's depredations were exposed, some MS&L shareholders pressed for another investigation into the company's affairs. Allegations of bias in awarding the contracts for the second Woodhead Tunnel were made, it was also suggested that Fowler had used railway staff on the development of his own property at New Holland. It was further intimated that the company had purchased land from the Chairman, Lord Yarborough, at a considerable financial advantage to himself. The accusation that the purchase of the Humber Ferries had been a fraudulent manipulation was the bitterest of all.

J.C. Jack was appointed by the shareholders to head a representative investigative committee. The committee met with the MS&L Directors on 14th February, 1850, stating they wished, '. . . to put an end to the agitation and ruin of the company's credit by a policy now pursued by a certain party out of doors', a desire shared by the Board. It was resolved that the membership of the Board should be changed, as an indication that the company had put its house in order; Lord Yarborough, however, was to remain as Chairman.

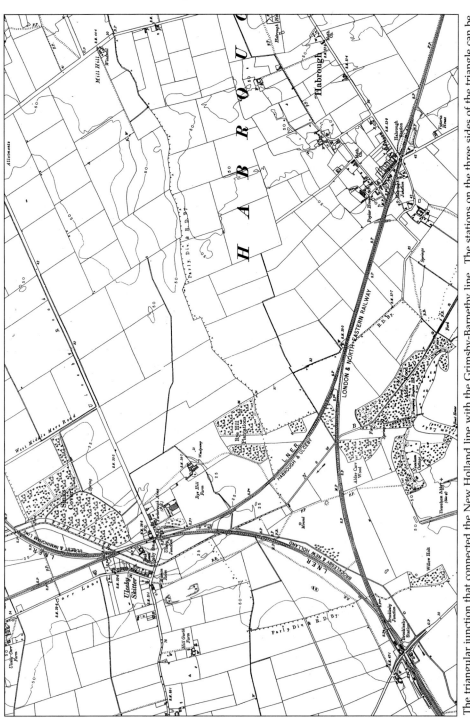

The triangular junction that connected the New Holland line with the Grimsby-Barnetby line. The stations on the three sides of the triangle can be seen (Brocklesby, Habrough and Ulceby). The New Holland line heads straight through Ulceby station. The line veering to the right is for Humber Road Junction and Immingham.

Reproduced from the 6″, 1932 Ordnance Survey Map

Chapter Four

Railways into New Holland

The section of railway between Grimsby and New Holland opened in conjunction with the East Lincolnshire Railway in 1848 (*see Chapter Three*). Stations along the line were at Great Coates, which was a superb example of GG&SJ architectural style - red brick Tudor style buildings, with stone features, in a cottage manner. Stallingborough station served a large scattered village on the banks of a rivulet two miles from the Humber. The station was situated about a mile south-west of the village and was provided with the basic facilities plus a cattle dock.

Habrough station was located 1½ miles south-west of the village. Alterations took place here in 1883, affecting the junction of the New Holland branch and the main lines. The revamping saw the abolition of the junction signal box and the rebuilding of the station in the MS&LR style and with staggered platforms. The junction was odd in that the line from Barnetby ran in parallel to the New Holland line as far as Habrough level crossing, before assuming the appearance of a normal junction; this was, no doubt, to alleviate the necessity for a new signal box at the junction. To prevent the imposition of speed restrictions on express traffic operating along the Barnetby line, the unusual step was taken of turning both lines out on reverse curves, instead of only the left-hand one. Habrough station was provided with sidings on each side of the running lines, the northern set serving a cattle dock and warehouse.

A further junction station was at Ulceby, where, in the early days when main line trains ran to New Holland, passengers for Grimsby changed trains. A refreshment room was authorised for the station by the MS&L Board in 1885. The Humber Commercial Railway opened on 29th June, 1910, and ran from Ulceby to Immingham Dock. Ulceby was an important station, built in true MS&L style; the signal box was a tall impressive structure which was, for several years, separated from the station by a temporary road bridge built to cope with increased road traffic from Immingham. With the opening of the A180 dual carriageway the bridge was removed and the level crossing restored. In the early days Ulceby was the post town for the surrounding area, the station master also running the post office.

Goxhill station displayed the tall chimneys and stone-pillared windows typical of the rest of the stations along the line. The station was sited in the village, itself something of a novelty for a Lincolnshire station, and was provided with the standard facilities with accommodation for dealing with cattle and coal. The signal box, at the south end of the layout, beyond the level crossing, also controlled traffic coming off, and going onto, the Immingham branch, after it opened in 1911.

Two further stations were opened at later dates. Thornton Curtis was a temporary halt, opening in November 1848. This was replaced by a more permanent arrangement, ½ mile nearer Goxhill, and named after the nearby ancient ruin, Thornton Abbey. The station master, Thomas Towers, was also publican of 'The Hunt' public house, in nearby Thornton Curtis. Two small signal boxes controlled level crossings at the north and south ends of the layout

An unidentified ex-GCR engine approaches Great Coates station with a train from Cleethorpes *c.* 1960. *Douglas Thompson*

Great Coates station looking towards Grimsby *c.* 1960. *Lens of Sutton*

Healing station, with a train approaching from the west, in 1960. The layout at this time was basically complete. *J.D. Munro*

Stallingborough station, crossing and signal box, the buildings here typical of the line. Notice the bell on the end of the station building. *Lens of Sutton*

Top: A neat looking Habrough station showing the buildings, footbridge, signal box and goods shed to good advantage. Looking towards Ulceby, note the staggered platforms.   *Author's Collection*

Centre: A dmu departs Habrough station in more modern times. The elegant GCR lamp standards have been replaced by characterless modern devices. The handsome seat still carries the legend 'Habrough' on its backrest.   *Lens of Sutton*

Right: Habrough Junction signal box, a standard GCR structure, seen here on 10th June, 1973.   *John Edgington*

A Class 'WD' 2-8-0, No. 90443, works a goods train through Ulceby station on 29th September, 1956. Apart from the signal box, from where this view was taken, this delightful example of New Holland line architecture has been replaced by bus shelters.

H.B. Priestley

A view from Ulceby station of the road crossing and imposing signal box.

Lens of Sutton

Ulceby station with the flyover in place on 4th May, 1975. The flyover was removed with the opening of the A180 dual carriageway and the road crossing restored. Here is seen the much modified waiting shelter on the east platform.

N.D. Mundy

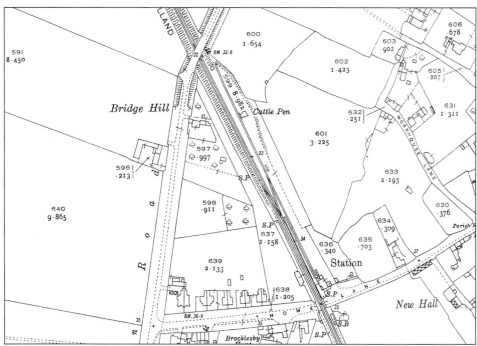

Goxhill station.   *Reproduced from the 25", 1932 Ordnance Survey Map*

A view of Goxhill station in GCR days. The wheel for operating the level crossing gates can be seen outlined in the signal box. Whether the ornate mangle standing on the platform has just been delivered and awaits collection or was part of the station equipment is not known!

Author's Collection

An early view of Goxhill station looking towards Thornton Abbey and giving a good idea of the layout. There is a wealth of signalling to be seen and the divergence of the Barton and Immingham line can just be discerned beyond the level crossing gates.   *B. Longbone Collection*

Goxhill station on 27th April, 1981. The station house is in private hands but very much intact. The only clue to the modernity of the photograph is the bus shelter on the up platform, the down platform shelter looks the worse for wear but is still in position.   *Yorston*

Thornton Abbey station with buildings at each end of the down platform seen here on 28th April, 1954. The small waiting shelter is just beyond the nearest building, a Victorian post box is provided in the near wall of the main building.   *H.C. Casserley*

The same situation looking towards Habrough. These buildings no longer exist, however the station nameboard survives now supported by posts. The pedestrian crossing at the end of the platform joins a footpath leading across a field to the remains of Thornton Abbey itself.

Lens of Sutton

respectively, this arrangement surviving until the road to the Abbey ruins was demoted to a footpath in 1885. In later years the remaining signal box was replaced by a ground frame operating the siding and crossover. The simple station buildings were supplemented by the provision of a cast-iron gents' urinal, standing in splendid isolation on the down side. Whether this ornate structure was provided because of the amount of passengers visiting the nearby ruins is unclear, but it is an amusing comment upon Victorian priorities. The huge LNER nameboards still survive at Thornton Abbey.

Approaching New Holland from Goxhill the train encountered Oxmarsh Junction signal box and level crossing. Early plans indicate a signal box on either side of the line here. The main route went straight on running east of a timber dock to an outer basin and Earles' shipyard. The passenger line curved westwards to Barrow Road signal box at one corner of a triangular layout which led west towards the Barton line and north into New Holland Town station. The engine shed was on the southern curve of the triangle, Barton Junction signal box at the west corner and New Holland Town box at the north corner. In the centre of the triangle was a reservoir for engine water. Between the dock and the passenger station were sidings for the handling of coal. These varied in number over the years between six and ten.

New Holland Town station had four roads through it, and originally had an overall roof. A fine red-brick building with a shallow slate roof and a decorative stone entrance stood on the down side, north of the signal box. The overall roof was replaced by the more familiar apex-roofed wooden canopy on the down side and a flat-roofed shelter on the up side. A footbridge stood at the southern end of the platforms.

The track out onto the piers was double, the buffer stops at the pier designated 107 miles 1 furlong and 70 chains from Manchester. The track along the pier was bounded on either side by an extension of the Town station platforms which eventually became the Pier station platforms. On the down side was a pedestrian walkway and on the up a wider vehicle access. At the pier end there were three roads, the middle one being used for the storage of wagons of coal for the ferries. A crane was provided for the transferring of goods to trollies for loading and off-loading the ferries.

Pier station buildings were wooden in construction, the more substantial, which had a canopy similar to the one at Town station, stood on the down side and included the refreshment rooms. A more modest building occupied the up side platform.

The Barton & New Holland Railway, authorised by an Act of 26th June, 1846, opened for traffic on 1st March, 1849. The initial service comprised six weekday and two Sunday trains in the down direction and five weekday and three Sunday trains in the reverse direction. The branch left a triangular junction at New Holland, the single line staff being held at Barton Junction signal box until its demise, at which point the duty became the responsibility of New Holland Town box. The line ran west for 3½ miles, to Barton, passing the tiny intermediate halt of Barrow Haven, 1½ miles out of New Holland. The halt was opened on 8th April, 1850 to serve a village two miles to the south. Here was a wooden platform with a shed-like waiting room and office and a station master's house, the occupant being the only person employed at this remote place. The original waiting shelter stood at the platform end, face-on to the

An immaculate Robinson 4-6-0, LNER class 'B3' No. 1498, approaches New Holland Town station with the 6.52 pm stopping train from Cleethorpes, on 18th April, 1947. This engine was named *Valour* in memory of Great Central railwaymen who died in World War I. The 'Yarborough Arms' can be seen in the background with the Barton line running across to the right and some interesting coaching stock in the siding.
H.C. Casserley

A picture with some over zealous touching up particularly on the right-hand side, showing engine No. 314 standing at New Holland Town station, *c.* 1906. No. 314 was a 2-4-0 built in 1873 and scrapped in May 1916.
Grimsby Public Library

Ex- GCR Atlantic No. 6083 takes a Cleethorpes-bound train through New Holland Town station at 1.52 pm on 10th May, 1946. No. 6083 was withdrawn a year later.
H.C. Casserley

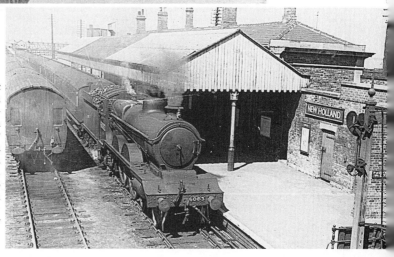

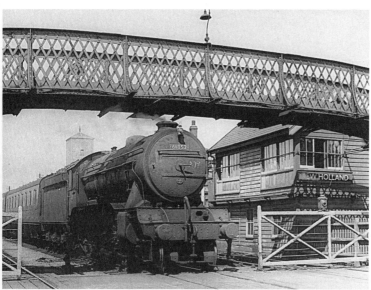

Left: An Immingham-based class 'K3' 2-6-0, No. 61852, alongside New Holland Town signal box in the 1960s with quite a rare view of the passenger footbridge south of the station.
A.J. Wickens

Below: An 'N5' class 0-6-2T has moved its train up the New Holland Town platform prior to departure to Barton. The coach nearest the engine is lettered 'New Holland-Barton'.
H.C. Casserley

An unidentified ex-GCR class 'J11' 0-6-0 stands in New Holland Town station on 22nd September, 1956. Opposite is a delightful view of the paraphernalia that occupied many station platforms at this time.
H. B. Priestley

The Pier, New Holland

A view of New Holland pier looking landwards and prior to the 1928 rebuilding by the LNER. A Sacré class '12A', No. 360, crosses from the down to the up line with a passenger train towards the end of the 1890s. *David Lee Photography*

A general view of New Holland pier taken on 28th June, 1928, a month after its reopening to traffic. The picture admirably conveys the bleakness of the place and one can quite easily imagine what it was like in windy, wet conditions. *Author's Collection*

One of a series of pictures taken a month after the reconstructed pier reopened for traffic. Class 'D9' 4-4-0 No. 6024, a popular local engine, stands in the middle road awaiting the arrival of a train from Cleethorpes. Built in 1902, No. 6024 was transferred from New Holland in May 1935, finishing up first at Kings Lynn, and finally Peterborough East. She became British Railways No. 62309 and was withdrawn in November 1949. *Author's Collection*

The eastern side of the pierhead station buildings seen on 28th June, 1928, and showing the intricate tracery of the roof structure to good advantage. This could be one of the coldest and most miserable places to wait for a train in England. *Author's Collection*

An Immingham-allocated class 'B1' 4-6-0 No. 61328 approaches New Holland Pier station with a train from Cleethorpes in July 1956. It was the introduction of this class of engine which saw the end of many of the ancient classes which had worked in the New Holland area for many years. *Author's Collection*

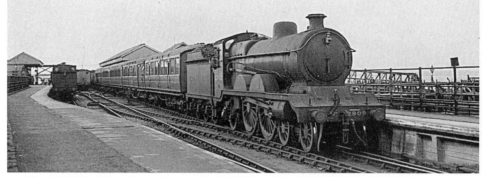

Class 'C4' No. 2909 waits to depart with the 7.40 pm New Holland Pier to Cleethorpes service on 9th June, 1947. A class 'N5' stands on the down line with the 7.53 pm train for Barton.

W.A. Camwell

Immingham-based class 'K2' 2-6-0 No. 61730 waits alongside New Holland pier signal box with a train for Cleethorpes in June 1952.

Author's Collection

In this view class 'A5' No. 69803 prepares to leave New Holland Pier station with a train of vintage stock for Barton.

David Lawrence

elements blowing of the Humber. A later, more spacious, pent-roof structure was sited on the opposite side, with its back firmly set against the river.

Barton station was a compact layout. The single platform housed the main buildings, comprising a two storey residence, flanked on either side by single storey offices and facilities; an awning ran from the eastern end of the buildings, stopping just short of the west end - opposite the platform stood a curved roofed, open goods shed. Also on this side, and built alongside a stream running at right angles to the railway, was a malt kiln and a bone mill. A long siding ran round towards the river, serving a cattle dock. In the early days a set of coal drops were provided in the yard, behind the main buildings. These were removed in June 1886, although part of the siding remained in place behind the platform. The branch ended at buffer stops at the west end of the platform, the layout having the look of an intermediate, rather than a terminus, station. The Timetable Appendix gave the following information about Barton:

When it is necessary for a freight train or light engine to run from New Holland to Barton-on-Humber whilst vehicles occupy the platform at Barton, New Holland must be advised and the enginemen must be notified at the time the train staff is handed to them at New Holland that vehicles are in the platform line. In such circumstances the driver must stop at the ground frame situated 90 yards east of Barton station. The station master at Barton must arrange for a man, with the necessary hand signals to be posted at the ground frame and exhibit a danger signal on all occasions when such conditions apply to ensure the driver stopping. During fog or falling snow the Hand-signalman must, in addition, place a detonator on the line.

To facilitate direct communication between Hull and Immingham via New Holland an Order for a light railway was obtained on 19th July, 1908. The original intention had been to construct a railway running from Barton, through Barrow, and crossing the Ulceby to New Holland line south of Goxhill station, and from there on to Immingham. The local press reported on 13th April, 1911,

Mr Sam Fay, with a staff of engineers, made a thorough inspection of the light railway from Immingham to Goxhill. This portion of the line has been completed for some time, even down to the laying out of the flower bed adjoining the new signal box at Goxhill. It is anticipated that the new line will be open for passengers within a few days. The agricultural interests of the neighbourhood it serves will benefit owing to the proximity of facilities for dealing with grain etc. which has previously had to be taken to Thornton and Ulceby stations. It will also give facilities for dairy farming, which have not been enjoyed in the past.

The remaining portion of the proposed light railway, from Goxhill through Barrow, joining up at Barton has not yet commenced, though of late much activity has been displayed along the route marked out for the project.

The *London Gazette*, on Tuesday 2nd May, 1911, contained the following, dated 'Board of Trade, Whitehall, May 1st',

The Light Railways Act: Barton and Immingham Light Railway (Extension of Time) Order: The Light Railway Commissioners have submitted to the Board of Trade for confirmation under the above mentioned Act, an Order made by them extending the periods limited by the Barton and Immingham Light Railway Order, 1908, for the compulsory purchase of lands and for the completion of the railway and works thereby authorised. Any objections to the confirmation of the Order should be addressed to the Assistant Secretary, (Railway Dept.) on or before 25th May next.

The neat little waiting shelter at Barrow Haven. Inside was a ticket office and a huge pot bellied stove in the middle of the waiting room. *J. Mann*

The small waiting room at Barrow Haven crouches with its back to the River Humber. The provision of lighting and seating on the platform would appear to be somewhat optimistic for such an isolated place. *Douglas Thompson*

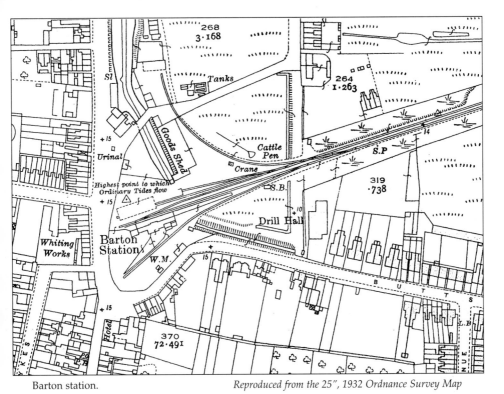

Barton station.   *Reproduced from the 25", 1932 Ordnance Survey Map*

A good selection of platform trolleys can be seen in this view of Barton station on 17th April, 1947. The train is the 9.33 am for New Holland, the nearest coach No. 51648.   *H.C. Casserley*

A 1954 view of Barton station seen from the road, the curved top of the goods shed is beyond the station buildings. None of this survives today, having been replaced by the ubiquitous bus shelter. *H.C. Casserley*

Barton station and goods shed seen from the buffer stops with some shunting in progress on 24th September, 1962. *Douglas Thompson*

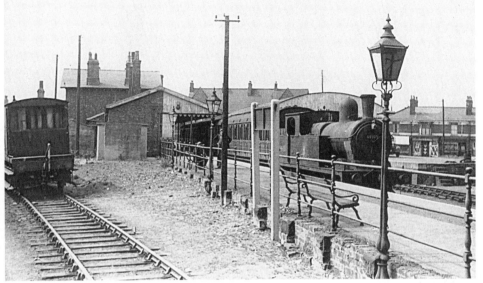

Class 'N5' 0-6-2T No. 69305 waits at Barton station with the 1.25 pm for New Holland, on 28th April, 1954. *H.C. Casserley*

Another view of Parker class 'N5' No. 69305 simmering quietly in the spring sunshine as she waits to take her train to New Holland in April 1954. The crew enjoy a few moments on the platform seat and appear to have the place to themselves. *H.C. Casserley*

A good view of Barton station from the buffer stops with rail car No. E79051 standing in the platform in July 1956. A nice contrast to the then very modern motive power is the elegant gas light standard on the platform. *Author's Collection*

A pleasant summer's day at Barton station with a dmu waiting to return to New Holland. A good view is given of the open sided goods shed and a shop blind proclaiming 'B. Briggs Fancy Draper'. *A.J. Wickens*

The Immingham-Goxhill section of the Barton and Immingham Railway opened on Monday 1st May, 1911, the first train departing Hull (Corporation Pier) at 5.20 am and arriving at Immingham (Western Jetty), at 6.10 am. The last train departed from Hull at 6.20 pm and arrived in Immingham at 7.25 pm. Trains from Immingham started at 6.15 am and arrived in Hull at 7.05 am. The last train set off from Immingham at 8.40 pm, reaching Hull at 9.35 pm. Six trains a day worked in both directions; workmen's weekly return tickets were issued on certain designated trains at reduced rates, from Hull, 2s. 6d., East Halton, 1s. and Killingholme, 6d.

The railway was built by Messrs Price, Reeves and Wills and, although it was termed a light railway, it in fact carried the same rolling stock as the rest of the GCR system; enough land had been enclosed to double the line if the need had arisen. The opening of the line was looked forward to by the population living between Goxhill and Immingham who anticipated their emancipation from the carriers' carts and drays, which had previously been their only means of transit from their out-of-the-way villages to the centres of population. Their delight was demonstrated in a practical way: at Killingholme the station was decked with flags, a large flag bore the message, 'Welcome'. The first train departed from Goxhill at just after 6.00 am, 36 passengers taking the journey to Immingham, at East Halton about the same number joined the train. They had only a five minute stay in Immingham, but they enjoyed the novelty of being passengers on the first trains. 'Even the horses, cattle and sheep seemed to take part in the rejoicing, for as the trains rattled past, they scampered away, either in delight or timidity'. About 80 tickets were collected at Immingham, most of which had been taken out by passengers anxious to have a look at the new dock; however, a few workmen availed themselves of the new service. On the Tuesday several people from Killingholme and East Halton made use of the service to visit Hull market.

No progress was made with the construction of the Barton and Immingham Railway between Goxhill and Barton, via Barrow. By November 1911 it was announced that the proposed extension of the North Lindsey Light Railway, from Wintringham to Barton, was to proceed, that the line was being surveyed and that markers were being put down along the route and they were not to be interfered with. Also coupled with this news was the idea that the Barton branch might be doubled.

The question of the continuation of the Barton and Immingham Railway was linked to this new proposal and it was postulated that the construction of the two new lines would form part of a direct link between Scunthorpe and Immingham, without going to New Holland. An alternative was to use the existing Barton line, which would allow access from Scunthorpe to Immingham and also to Hull, via New Holland. The doubling of the Barton branch would enable an accelerated service. The *Hull Times*, of 25th November, 1911, commented,

This, with the acquisition of new ferry steamers, will make communications between North Lincolnshire and Hull considerably better than at the present time. The question naturally arises whether Hull deserves any better facilities than at present with North Lincolnshire? If it values the Lincolnshire trade - which, if encouraged, will come in increasing volume - let it show its earnestness by stretching out its hands, and giving better facilities in the matter of landing both passengers and cattle. The present slopes are as antiquated as Mount Ararat and Noah's descent out of the Ark.

Men on their way to or from work on the construction of the Barton & Immingham Railway, transported in d u m b - b u f f e r e d contractor's wagons specially adapted for the job.
B. Longbone Collection

Left: A nice little tableau, East Halton Halt on 28th April, 1954. A primitive waiting shelter flanked by two elegant lamp standards and seats, but hardly likely to win any awards in the 'Best Kept Station' competition. *H.C. Casserley*

Below: There was definitely a light railway appearance to Killingholme Admiralty Platform with its wooden platform and primitive passenger facilities.
B. Longbone Collection

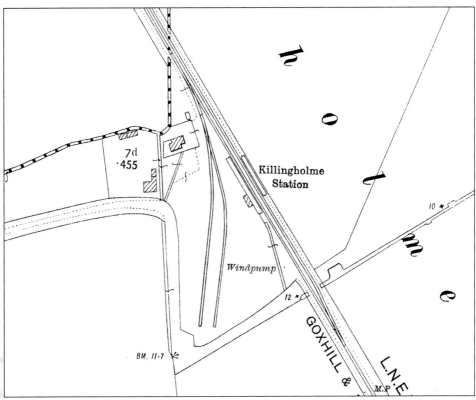

Killingholme station.   *Reproduced from the 25", 1932 Ornance Suvey Map*

The sparse facilities afforded at Killingholme station are apparent in this September 1962 view. The station closed the following year.   *D. Thompson*

BARTON & IMMINGHAM LIGHT RAILWAY.

On MONDAY, 1st MAY, 1911,

THE NEW RAILWAY

Between

GOXHILL & IMMINGHAM

**will be opened and a Service of Trains
will run as under:—**

WEEK DAYS.

	a.m.	a.m.	a.m.	p.m.	p.m.	p.m.
Hull (Corporation Pier) dep.	5 20A	8 25	11 50	1 30	5 20	6 30
New Holland .... arr.	5 40	8 45	12 10	1 50	5 40	6 50
Barton-on-Humber...dep.	...	8 20	11 40	1 0	5 15	6 35
New Holland .... ,,	5 45	8 50	12 15	1 55	5 45	7 0
Goxhill ....,.................. ,,	5 50	8 55	12 20	2 0	5 50	7 5
East Halton .... ,,	5 58A	9 3	12 28	2 8	5 58	7 13
Killingholme .... ,,	6 4A	9 9	12 34	2 14	6 4	7 19
Immingham ....arr. (Western Jetty)	6 10	9 15	12 40	2 20	6 10	7 25

	a.m.	a.m.	B p.m.	B p.m.	B p.m.	B p.m.
Immingham ....dep. (Western Jetty)	6 15	10 0	12 50	3 15	6 23	8 40
Killingholme .... ,,	6 21	10 6	12 56	3 21	6 29	8 46
East Halton .... ,,	6 27	10 12	1 2	3 27	6 35	8 52
Goxhill .... ,,	6 35	10 20	1 10	3 35	6 43	9 0
New Holland ....arr.	6 40	10 25	1 15	3 40	6 48	9 6
Barton-on-Humber... ,,	7 35	11 5	1 35	4*46	7 37	9 20
New Holland ....dep.	6 45	10 48	1 20	3 45	7 5	9 15
Hull (Corporation Pier) arr.	7 5	11 8	1 40	4 5	7 25	9 35

* Thursdays only.

WORKMEN'S WEEKLY RETURN TICKETS

**will be issued to IMMINGHAM (Western Jetty) by trains marked A,
available for return by trains marked B, at the following fares:—**

	s. d.			s. d.
Hull (C.P.)	2 6	East Halton	...	1 0

Killingholme ... 6d.

Marylebone Station,
London, April, 1911.

BY ORDER.

Knapp, Drewett & Sons Ltd., 30, Victoria Street, Westminster, and Kingston-on-Thames.—G.C. 1211.

As it turned out neither railway extension was built, the Barton branch and the Barton and Immingham Railway both remaining single track.

At this time the Admiralty proposed the establishment of an oil fuel terminal, with eight large reservoirs facing the river, about two miles above Immingham Dock, a short distance above the entrance to Killingholme Haven. Also in the proposal was a jetty, extending out into the river, 800 ft in length and 10 ft wide, with a 'T' head, 200 ft long. A naval seaplane base was established here and Killingholme Admiralty Platform opened to serve the complex. This was a simple affair with a wooden platform, basic waiting shelter, a seat and nameboard. Although tickets were issued to Admiralty Platform none was ever issued *from* it, however it remained in regular use until closure of the line to passengers on 17th June, 1963.

Other stations on the line were at Immingham, the original station was Immingham Western Jetty, and consisted of a wooden platform and minuscule wooden ticket office. This was later replace by a more substantial arrangement built close to the Entrance Lock, incorporating a long curved platform, an interesting simple storey structure with tall brick-built chimneys at each end, a brick-built ladies toilet and next to that, a single storey brick-built, and rather ugly, flat roof structure. An old grounded coach body stood near the nameboard.

Killingholme station was a very basic affair, consisting of a short wooden platform with a pent-roof metal shelter and a seat. At East Halton a similar set-up existed except that here there were two platforms, no doubt in anticipation of the line being doubled.

As from 31st December, 1912, the Barton and Immingham was vested in the Humber Commercial Railway and leased to the Great Central Railway under that company's Act of the same year.

The original station on the west side of Immingham Dock. The replacement station was built to the east of Western Jetty station and was named 'Immingham Dock'.

Grimsby Public Library

Table 82 HULL, NEW HOLLAND, GRIMSBY, and CLEETHORPES

Week Days

Miles		a.m From Penistone	a.m From Manchester	a.m	a.m From Lincoln	a.m From Scunthorpe	a.m From Doncaster	a.m	a.m B From Sheffield	a.m C From Leeds	D	a.m Y From Rotherham and Masboro'
	Hull (Corp. Pier)* dep	..	..	..				7 35			9 20	
—	New Holland Pier dep			6 27				8 3			9 48	
	New Holland Town "			6 30				8 6			..	
2¼	Goxhill			6 35				8 12			..	
3¾	Thornton Abbey			6 39				8 16			..	
6¼	Ulceby			6 45				8 22			..	
7½	Brocklesby arr			..	6 51	7 33	7 54	..			..	
	Brocklesby dep	..	..	..	6 52	7 34	7 55	..			..	
8	Habrough	..	5 29	6 49	6 57	7 39	8§ 2	8d30	..	..	..	
12	Stallingborough	..	..	6 56	7 4	7 46	8 9	8 37	..	..	..	
13	Healing	..	..	6 59	7 7	7 49	8 12	8 40	..	..	..	
14½	Great Coates	..	..	7 2	7 10	7 52	8 15	8 43	..	..	..	
16½	Grimsby Town arr	5 23	5 42	7 7	7 15	7 57	8 20	8 48	9 26	..	1013	10 14
	Grimsby Town dep	5 36	6 1	7 10	7 19	8 1	8 25	8 52	9 30	..	1016	10 18
17½	Grimsby Docks	5A43	6d9	7 15	7§25	8 6	8§31	8 57	9A37	10A8	..	10§24
18	New Clee	..	6 13	7 20	..	..	..	9 2	..	..	..	..
19½	Cleethorpes arr	5 50	6 17	7 24	7 36	8 12	8 42	9 6	9 44	1015	1026	10 30

	a.m From Sheffield	a.m	a.m From Lincoln	a.m J From Leicester	a.m E From Doncaster	a.m S From Doncaster	a.m K From Bradford	a.m L From Leeds	a.m	p.m S From Retford
Hull (Corp. Pier)* dep	..	9 20	..						11 5	
New Holland Pier dep	..	9 55							11 50	
New Holland Town "	..	9 58							11 53	
Goxhill	..	10 4							11 58	
Thornton Abbey	..	10 8							..	
Ulceby		10§14							12 7	
Brocklesby arr		..	1020		10 41	1048			..	1241
Brocklesby dep		..	1021		10 42	1049			..	1242
Habrough		10 19	1027	..	10 45	1055	..	..	12 12	..
Stallingborough		..	1034	..	..	..	..	..	..	..
Healing		..	1037	..	..	..	..	..	12 20	..
Great Coates		..	1040	..	..	..	..	..	12 24	..
Grimsby Town arr	1021	10 33	1045	..	11 0	11 7	1128	1146	12 29	1256
Grimsby Town dep	1026	10 35	1050	..	11 5	1112	1132	1150	12 32	1258
Grimsby Docks	1031	10§41	1054	11A3	11 10	1117	..	..	12§38	1 3
New Clee	..	10 45	1059	..	..	..	..	..	12 42	..
Cleethorpes arr	1037	10 49	11 3	1110	11 21	1128	1142	12 0	12 46	1 9

	p.m From Manchester	p.m From Retford	p.m From Lincoln	S	p.m	p.m From Doncaster	p.m	p.m N From Manchester	p.m From Sheffield	p.m From Doncaster
Hull (Corp. Pier)* dep		..	..	1 15	2 0		2 0		..	
New Holland Pier dep				1 52	2 30		2 44			
New Holland Town "				1 55	2 33		2 48			
Goxhill				2 0	2 39		2 53			
Thornton Abbey				2 4	..		2 57			
Ulceby				2 11	2 48		3 3			
Brocklesby arr		1 27		..	2 51		..			4 17
Brocklesby dep	..	1 28	..	..	2 52		..		..	4 18
Habrough	1 11	1 33	2 10	2 16	To Lincoln	3 1	3 8	..	..	4 24
Stallingborough	..	1 40	..	2 23		..	3 15	..	..	4 31
Healing	..	1 43	..	2 26		..	3 18	..	..	4 34
Great Coates	..	1 46	..	2 29		..	3 21	..	..	4 37
Grimsby Town arr	1 23	1 51	2 22	2 34		3 14	3 26	3 35	4 16	4 42
Grimsby Town dep	1 28	1 55	2 25	2 39		3 17	3 29	3 40	4 22	4 47
Grimsby Docks	1 33	2 0	2 30	2§45		3 22	3 34	3A47	4§28	4§55
New Clee	..	2 4	2 35	2 49	..	3 29	3 44	..	..	..
Cleethorpes arr	1 39	2 8	2 39	2 53	..	3 33	3 48	3 55	4 34	5 3

Week Days—continued

	P	p.m	E From Scunthorpe	p.m From Leeds	p.m From Lincoln	p.m	p.m From Sheffield (Manchester (C.) Sats only)	p.m From Doncaster	p.m From King's Cross
Hull (Corp. Pier)* dep	4 30	4 30		..	..	5 30			..
New Holland Pier dep	5 0	5 7				6 10			
New Holland Town "	..	5 10				6 13			
Goxhill	..	5 16				6 19			
Thornton Abbey	..	5 20				6 24			
Ulceby	..	5 26				6 31			
Brocklesby arr	..	..	6 1		6§24	..		7 4	
Brocklesby dep	..	..	6 2	..	6§25	..		7 5	
Habrough	..	5§32	6 7	..	6 29	6 36		7 10	
Stallingborough	..	5 39	..	..	..	..		7 17	
Healing	..	5 42	6 15	..	..	6 44		7 20	..
Great Coates	..	5 46	..	..	..	6 48		7 23	..
Grimsby Town arr	5 25	5 51	6 22	6 31	6 41	6 53	7 8	7 28	7 47
Grimsby Town dep	5 28	5 56	6 24	6 34	6 45	6 56	7 13	7 33	7 57
Grimsby Docks	..	6d4	6 29	6 39	6 50	7 1	7 18	7 38	8 2
New Clee	..	6 12	6 33	..	6 54	..	..	7 42	..
Cleethorpes arr	5 38	6 16	6 37	6 45	6 58	7 12	7 24	7 46	8 9

	p.m	p.m S	p.m From Manchester	E From Birmingham (New St.)	p.m	p.m From Lincoln	p.m From Doncaster	R	
Hull (Corp. Pier)* dep	7 20		..		8 50	..		10 5	..
New Holland Pier dep	7 50	..			9 30			1035	..
New Holland Town "	7 53	..			9 33			1037	..
Goxhill	7 58	..			9 38			1042	..
Thornton Abbey	8 2	..			9 42			1046	..
Ulceby	8 8	..			9 48			1052	..
Brocklesby arr	..	..			..		10 8	..	..
Brocklesby dep	..	..	..		..	..	10 9	..	..
Habrough	8 12	8 38	8A48	9 0	9 52	10 4	1014	1056	..
Stallingborough	8 19	..	..	..	9 59	..	1021	11 3	..
Healing	8 22	..	..	..	10 2	..	1024	11 6	..
Great Coates	8 25	..	..	..	10 5	..	1027	11 9	..
Grimsby Town arr	8 30	8 50	9 0	9 12	1010	1016	1032	1114	..
Grimsby Town dep	8 34	8 54	9 5	9 16	1012	1020	1037	1116	..
Grimsby Docks	8A41	8 59	9 10	9 21	1017	1025	1042	1120	..
New Clee	..	..	..	..	..	..	..	..	..
Cleethorpes arr	8 51	9 5	9 16	9 27	1023	1031	1053	1126	..

Sundays

	a.m From Manchester	a.m	a.m. From Doncaster	a.m	a.m From Sheffield	a.m	p.m
Hull (Corp. Pier)* dep	..	7 40		1025		1155	1 40
New Holland Pier dep		8 15		1110		1240	2 15
New Holland Town "		8 18		..		1243	2 18
Goxhill		8 23		..		1248	2 23
Thornton Abbey		8 27		..		1252	2 27
Ulceby		8 33		..		1258	2 33
Brocklesby arr		..	10 53	..	1139	..	..
Brocklesby dep	..	..	10 54	..	1140	..	..
Habrough	..	8 37	10 58	..	1145	1 2	2 38
Stallingborough	..	8 44	11 5	..	1153	1 9	..
Healing	..	8 47	11 8	..	1156	1 12	..
Great Coates	..	8 51	11 12	..	12 0	1 16	..
Grimsby Town arr	6 1	8 56	11 16	..	12 5	1 21	2 51
Grimsby Town dep	6 23	8 59	11 21	..	1210	1 29	2 54
Grimsby Docks	6d31	9 4	11A30	..	1215	1 34	2 59
New Clee	..	..	..	..	..	..	..
Cleethorpes arr	6 38	9 11	11 37	1146	1222	1 41	3 6

	p.m From Doncaster	p.m	p.m From Doncaster	p.m	p.m From Sheffield	p.m From King's Cross	
Hull (Corp. Pier)* dep		4 20		7 5		..	..
New Holland Pier dep		4 55		7 40		..	..
New Holland Town "		4 58		7 43		..	..
Goxhill		5 3		7 48		..	..
Thornton Abbey		5 7		7 52		..	..
Ulceby		5 13		7 58		..	..
Brocklesby arr	4 40	..	7 16	..	9 48		..
Brocklesby dep	4 41	..	7 17	..	9 49		..
Habrough	4 46	5 17	7 22	8 2	9 54		..
Stallingborough	..	5 24	7 29	8 9	10 2		..
Healing	4 54	5 27	7 32	8 12	10 5		..
Great Coates	4 57	5 31	7 36	8 16	10 9		..
Grimsby Town arr	5 2	5 36	7 41	8 21	1014	1025	..
Grimsby Town dep	5 7	5 39	7 45	8 24	1017	1035	..
Grimsby Docks	5§14	5 44	7 50	8 29	1022	1039	..
New Clee	..	..	..	..	..	..	..
Cleethorpes arr	5 21	5 51	7 57	8 36	1029	1047	..

A Arr. 4 minutes *earlier*
B Sats. only. Commences 18th June
C Except Fris. and Sats. Runs 27th June to 1st September inclusive
D Tues., Weds., and Thurs. Runs 19th July to 1st Sept. inclusive
d Arr. 5 minutes *earlier*
E Except Saturdays
J Sats. only. Runs 4th June to 17th September inclusive
K Sats. only. Runs 2nd July to 3rd September inclusive
L Sats. only. Runs 2nd July to 17th September inclusive
N Sats. only. Runs 11th June to 10th September inclusive
P Tues. only. Runs 28th June to 6th September inclusive
R Thurs. and Sats.
S or § Saturdays only
Y Sats. only. Commences 4th June
§ Arr. 3 minutes *earlier*

***The times shown leaving Hull are those at which the Ferry leaves the Corporation Pier, and passengers having to book must present themselves at the Booking Office in Nelson Street at least three minutes before times advertised for departure of Ferry otherwise passengers cannot be booked; and should any delay from low tides or other cause beyond the Executive's control occur in the passage of the Ferry the passengers must proceed from New Holland by the next available train.**

For **OTHER TRAINS** between New Holland and Goxhill, see Table 85.

Table 82—continued CLEETHORPES, GRIMSBY, NEW HOLLAND, and HULL

Week Days

Miles		a.m To Doncaster	a.m	a.m To Lincoln	Z	a.m To Retford	a.m	a.m To Doncaster	T	a.m To Lincoln	a.m To King's Cross
—	Cleethorpes dep	5 46	6 10	6 25	6 52	7 10	7 48	8 0	8 35	8 50	8 57
1¼	New Clee	5 50	6 14	6 29	..	7 14	7 52	..	..	..	..
2¼	Grimsby Docks	5d59	6§21	6§36	7§ 1	7 20	7 58	8b10	8 43	8 57	9b7
3¼	Grimsby Town arr	6 2	6 24	6 39	7 4	7 23	8 1	8 13	8 46	9 0	9 10
	Grimsby Town dep	6 6	6 26	6 42	7 8	7 27	8 5	8 16	8 50	9 3	9 23
5¼	Great Coates	6 11	6 31	6 48	..	7 32	8 10	..	8 55		
6¾	Healing	6 14	6 34	6 52	..	7 35	8 13	..	8 58		
7¾	Stallingborough	..	6 37	6 55	..	7 38	..	..	..		
11¼	Habrough	6 24	6§47	7 4	7 22	7 46	8 23	8§32	9 7		
13¼	Brocklesby arr	6 27	..	7 7	..	7 49	..	8 34	9 10		
	Brocklesby dep	6 28	..	7 8	..	7 50	..	8 36	9 11		
13	Ulceby		6 51		..		8 27		..	..	
15¼	Thornton Abbey		6 58		..		8 33		..	..	
17¼	Goxhill		7 4		..		8§39		..	..	
19½	New Holland Town arr		7 8		..		8 43		..	..	..
	New Holland Pier "		7 13		..		8 47		..	..	..
22½	Hull (Corp. Pier) arr		7 40		..		9 25		..	..	..

		a.m To Leeds	A To Sheffield	P	a.m To Manchester	a.m	a.m To Doncaster	a.m To Sheffield	S	noon To Lincoln
Cleethorpes dep	..	9 10	9 20	9 30	9 45	9 53	10 13	11 45	1152	12 0
New Clee	..	..	..	..	..	9 57	10 17	..	1156	..
Grimsby Docks	..	9 17	..	..	9 53	10 2	10b25	11b55	12 2	12b10
Grimsby Town arr	..	9 20	9 30	9 40	9 56	10 5	10 28	11 58	12 5	12 13
Grimsby Town dep	..	9 22	9 34	9 44	10 0	10 8	10 34	12 1	12 8	12 17
Great Coates	..		..	..		10 13	10 39	..	1213	12 22
Healing	..		..	..		10 16	10 42	..	1216	12 26
Stallingborough	..		..	..		10 20	10 45	..	1220	12 30
Habrough	..		..	..		10 29	10 53	12§16	1229	12 39
Brocklesby arr	..			..		..	10 56	12 19	..	12 42
Brocklesby dep	..			..		..	10 57	12 20	..	12 43
Ulceby	..			..		10 33			1233	
Thornton Abbey	..	..		..	..	10 39			1239	
Goxhill	..	..		..	..	10§45			1243	
New Holland Town arr	..	..	..	..	..	10 49			1247	
New Holland Pier "	..	..	..	10 9	..	10 53			1250	
Hull (Corp. Pier) arr	..	..	..	1040	..	11 25			1 20	

		p.m To Doncaster	p.m	J To Leicester	K To Bradford	U To Sheffield	L To Leeds	p.m To Retford	p.m	A To Sheffield
Cleethorpes dep	..	12 38	1 7	1 20	1 30	2 5	2 14	2 24	2 34	2 45
New Clee	..	12 42	..	..	..	..	..	..	2 38	..
Grimsby Docks	..	12d51	1b17	1b30	..	..	..	2b34	2 44	..
Grimsby Town arr	..	12 54	1 20	..	1 40	2 14	2 24	2 37	2 47	2 54
Grimsby Town dep	..	12 57	1 23	..	1 44	2 18	2 28	2 42	2 49	2 58
Great Coates	..	1 2	..	..	..	..	..	..	2 54	..
Healing	..	1 5	1 30					..	2 57	
Stallingborough	..	1 8	1 33					..	3 0	
Habrough	..	1 17	1 42					2 56	3 8	
Brocklesby arr	..	..	..					..	..	
Brocklesby dep	..		..						..	
Ulceby	..		1 46						3 12	
Thornton Abbey	..		1 52						3 18	
Goxhill	..		1 56	..	..	..	..		3 22	..
New Holland Town arr	..		2 0	..	..	..	..		3 26	..
New Holland Pier "	..		2 4	..	..	..	..		3 29	..
Hull (Corp. Pier) arr	..	..	2 35	..	..	..	..	..	4 0	..

Week Days—continued

	p.m To Penistone	p.m	p.m	S To Lincoln	E To Lincoln	S To Retford	Y To Rotherham and Masboro'	p.m To Doncaster	B To Sheffield
Cleethorpes dep	2 56	3 27	4 52	5 13	5 18	5 39	5 50	6 1	6 30
New Clee	..	..	4 56	5 17	5 22	5 43	..	..	..
Grimsby Docks	3§5	3 34	5‡5	5b25	5b30	5 49	..	6‡14	6b40
Grimsby Town arr	3 8	3 37	5 8	5 28	5 33	5 52	5 59	6 17	6 43
Grimsby Town dep	3 17	3 40	5 10	5 33	5 38	5 55	6 3	6 21	6 47
Great Coates	..	3 45	5 15	5 39	5 44	..	..	6 26	..
Healing	..	3 48	5 19	5 43	5 48	..		6 30	
Stallingborough	..	3 51	5 23	5 47	5 52	..		..	
Habrough	3b33	3 59	5 35	5b58	6b3	6 6		..	
Brocklesby arr	3 36	..	..	6 1	6 6	6 9		..	
Brocklesby dep	3 37	..	..	6 2	6 7	6 10		..	
Ulceby		4 3	5 39						..
Thornton Abbey		..	5 45						..
Goxhill		4 12	5 50						..
New Holland Town arr		4 16	5 54						..
New Holland Pier "		4 20	5 57						..
Hull (Corp. Pier) arr		4 50	6 30				..	..	..

	p.m To Manchester	D	p.m	C To Leeds	p.m	p.m		
Cleethorpes dep	6 40	6 48	6 53	7 32	8 22	10 0	..	..
New Clee	..	..	6 57	..	..	..	..	..
Grimsby Docks	6d51	6 56	7§4	7§41	8 29	10 8	..	..
Grimsby Town arr	6 54	..	7 7	..	8 32	1011	..	..
Grimsby Town dep	7 2	..	7 10	..	8 35	1014	..	..
Great Coates	..	..	7 15	..	8 40	1019	..	..
Healing	..	..	7 19		8 43	1022	..	..
Stallingborough	..	..	7 22		8 46	1025	..	..
Habrough	7b21	..	7 31		8 54	1033	..	..
Brocklesby arr		..	..		..	..	..	..
Brocklesby dep		..	..		..	..	..	..
Ulceby		..	7 35		8 58	1037	..	..
Thornton Abbey		..	7 41		9§4	1043	..	..
Goxhill		..	7 45	..	9 7	1047	..	..
New Holland Town arr		..	7 49	..	9 11	1051	..	..
New Holland Pier "		7 25	7 52	..	9 14	..	..	..
Hull (Corp. Pier) arr	..	..	8 20	..	9 45	..	..	..

Sundays

	a.m To Doncaster	a.m	a.m To Doncaster	a.m To King's Cross	a.m To Sheffield	a.m		p.m
Cleethorpes dep	5 39	7 0	8 15	8 50	9 16	1118	..	3 35
New Clee	..	..	..	..	..	..	..	..
Grimsby Docks	5 46	7 7	8 23	8 58	9d27	1125	..	3 43
Grimsby Town arr	5 49	7 10	8 26	9 1	9 30	1128	..	3 46
Grimsby Town dep	5 57	7 14	8 30	9 15	9 35	1136	..	3 49
Great Coates	..	7 19	..		9 40	1141	..	3 53
Healing	6 4	7 23	8 37		9 44	1144	..	3 56
Stallingborough	..	7 27	..		9 48	1148	..	4 0
Habrough	6 15	7 36	8 47		9 57	1155	..	4 7
Brocklesby arr	..	..	..		10 0	..	..	..
Brocklesby dep	..	..	..		10 1	..	..	..
Ulceby		7 40				1159	..	4 11
Thornton Abbey		7 46				12 5	..	4 17
Goxhill		7 50				12 9	..	4 21
New Holland Town arr		7 54		..		1213	..	4 25
New Holland Pier "		7 57		..		1216	..	4 28
Hull (Corp. Pier) arr	..	8 45	..	..		1255	..	5 20

	p.m To Sheffield	p.m To Doncaster	p.m	p.m To Sheffield	p.m	p.m	
Cleethorpes dep	4 20	5 50	6 15	6 25	6 35	9 40	..
New Clee	..	..	..	..	..	..	..
Grimsby Docks	4 29	6b0	6 23	6 33	6 42	9 47	..
Grimsby Town arr	4 32	6 3	6 26	6 36	6 45	9 50	..
Grimsby Town dep	4 37	6 8	6 29	6 41	6 48	9 53	..
Great Coates	4 42	6 13	..	..	6 53	9 58	..
Healing	4 46	6 18	..	..	6 56	10 1	..
Stallingborough	4 49	6 22	..	..	7 0	10 5	..
Habrough	4 57	6b33	..	6§57	7 7	1012	..
Brocklesby arr	5 0	6 36	..	7 1	..	..	..
Brocklesby dep	5 1	6 37	..	7 3	..	..	..
Ulceby			..		7 11	1016	..
Thornton Abbey			..		7 17	1022	..
Goxhill			..		7 21	1026	..
New Holland Town arr			..		7 25	1030	..
New Holland Pier "			6 55		7 28	..	..
Hull (Corp. Pier) arr			..		8 0	..	..

A Sats. only. Runs 18th June to 10th September inclusive
B Sats. only. Commences 18th June
b Arr. 4 minutes *earlier*
C Except Fris. and Sats. Runs 27th June to 1st September inclusive
D Tues., Weds., and Thurs. Runs 19th July to 1st Sept. inclusive
d Arr. 5 minutes *earlier*
E Except Saturdays
J Sats. only. Runs 4th June to 17th September inclusive
K Sats. only. Runs 2nd July to 3rd September inclusive
L Sats. only. Runs 2nd July to 17th September inclusive
P Tues. only. Runs 28th June to 6th September inclusive
S or § Saturdays only
T To Sheffield (to Manchester (Cen.) on Saturdays)
U Sats. only. Runs 9th July to 10th September inclusive
Y Saturdays only. Commences 4th June
Z Thro' train Cleethorpes to Birmingham (New St.) (to Bournemouth (West) on Sats.)
‡ Arr. 6 minutes *earlier*
§ Arr. 3 minutes *earlier*

For **OTHER TRAINS** between Goxhill and New Holland, see Table 85

Table 83 HULL, NEW HOLLAND, and BARTON-ON-HUMBER

Week Days

Miles		a.m	a.m		a.m	a.m	a.m	a.m	a.m	noon S		E	S	p.m	p.m	p.m	p.m	p.m	p.m	p.m	R
	Hull (Corp'tion Pier)* dep	..	..	..	7 35	8 25	9 20	1010	11 5		..	1210	1210	1 15	2 0	3 30	4 30	5 30	7 20	8 50	10 5
	New Holland (Pier).. arr	..	..	..	7 55	8 45	9 40	1030	1125	..	..	1230	1230	1 35	2 20	3 50	4 50	5 50	7 40	9 10	1025
—	New Holland Pier.... dep	6 34	7 13	..	..	8 55	..	1050	..	12 0	..	1240	1250	2 5	..	4 5	..	6 0	7 56	9 20	1053
	New Holland Town... "	6 36	7 16	..	..	8 58	..	1053	..	12 3	..	1243	1253	2 8	..	4 8	..	6 3	7 59	9 23	1055
1½	Barrow Haven	6 40	7 20	..	..	9 2	..	1058	..	12 7	..	1247	1257	2 12	..	4 12	..	6 7	8 4	9 25	1059
3½	Barton-on-Humber.... arr	6 45	7 25	..	..	9 7	..	11 5	..	1212	..	1252	1 2	2 17	..	4 17	..	6 12	8 9	9 33	11 4

Sundays

	a.m	a.m	a.m	a.m		p.m	p.m	p.m	p.m	
Hull (Corp'tion Pier)* dep	7 40	9 5	1025	1155	..	1 40	4 20	5 40	7 5	..
New Holland (Pier).. arr	8 0	9 25	1045	1215	..	2 0	4 40	6 0	7 25	..
New Holland Pier.... dep	8 32	9 45	11 2	1233	..	..	4 50	6 15	7 45	..
New Holland Town... "	8 35	9 48	11 5	1235	..	..	4 53	6 18	7 47	..
Barrow Haven	8 39	9 52	11 9	1239	..	..	4 57	6 22	7 51	..
Barton-on-Humber.... arr	8 44	9 57	1114	1244	..	..	5 2	6 27	7 56	..

Week Days

Miles		a.m	a.m	a.m		a.m	a.m	a.m	a.m		S	p.m	p.m	p.m	p.m		p.m	p.m	p.m	p.m	R	
	Barton-on-Humber.... dep	6 15	6 50	7 50	..	..	9 44	..	1135	..	1230	..	1 25	3 10	..	..	5 37	..	7 30	8 53	1010	..
2	Barrow Haven	6 20	6 55	7 55	..	..	9 49	..	1140	..	1235	..	1 30	3 15	..	..	5 42	..	7 35	8 58	1015	..
3¾	New Holland Town.. arr	6 24	6 59	7 59	..	..	9 53	..	1144	..	1239	..	1 34	3 19	..	..	5 46	..	7 39	9 2	1019	..
	New Holland Pier.... "	6 26	7 1	8 3	..	..	9 56	..	1148	..	1242	..	1 37	3 22	..	..	..	..	7 42	9 5	1022	..
—	New Holland (Pier).. dep	..	7 20	8 25	..	9 5	1020	11 5	12 5	..	..	1 0	2 15	3 40	4 30	..	..	6 10	8 0	9 25	..	..
6¾	Hull (Corporation Pier) arr	..	7 40	8 45	..	9 25	1040	1125	1225	..	..	1 20	2 35	4 0	4 50	..	..	6 30	8 20	9 45	..	..

Sundays

	a.m	a.m	a.m		p.m	p.m	p.m	p.m	p.m	
Barton-on-Humber.... dep	8 5	9 23	1038	..	1216	..	4 30	5 50	7 21	..
Barrow Haven	..	9 28	1043	..	1221	..	4 35	5 55	7 26	..
New Holland Town.. arr	8 12	9 32	1048	..	1225	..	4 39	5 59	7 30	..
New Holland Pier.... "	8 15	9 35	1050	..	1227	..	4 42	6 4	7 33	..
New Holland (Pier).. dep	8 25	9 45	1110	..	1235	2 30	5 0	6 20	7 40	..
Hull (Corporation Pier) arr	8 45	10 5	1130	..	1255	2 50	5 20	6 40	8 0	..

E Except Saturdays S or § Saturdays only R Thursdays and Saturdays * See note below

Table 85   NEW HOLLAND and IMMINGHAM

	Miles		a.m		a.m		p.m		p.m		H		
		Week Days only											
New Holland { Pier dep		Pier dep	6 40	..	8 50	..	1 45	..	4 0	..	6 17	..	
		Town ..	6 43	..	8 53	..	1 48	..	4 3	..	6 20	..	
Goxhill	2¼		6 48	..	8 58	..	1 53	..	4 8	..	6 25	..	
East Halton Halt	5		6 56	..	9 6	..	2 1	..	4 16	..	6 33	..	
Killingholme	7¼		7 4	..	9 14	..	2 9	..	4 24	..	6 41	..	
Immingham Dock arr	9¼		7 10	..	9 20	..	2 15	..	4 30	..	6 47	..	

	Miles		a.m		S		E		p.m		p.m		H	
		Week Days only												
Immingham Doc . dep			7 43	..	12 0	..	1210	..	2 45	..	5 15	..	7 5	..
Killingholme	2		7 49	..	12 6	..	1216	..	2 51	..	5 21	..	7 11	..
East Halton Halt	4¼		7 57	..	12 14	..	1224	..	2 59	..	5 29	..	7 19	..
Goxhill	7¼		S410	..	1247	..	1232	..	3 7	..	5 37	..	7 27	..
New Holland { Town	9¼	Town	8 15	..	12 32	..	1237	..	3 12	..	5 42	..	7 32	..
		Pier arr	8 18	..	12 35	..	1240	..	3 15	..	5 44	..	7 35	..

d Arr. 5 mins. *earlier*
E Except Saturdays
H Except Fridays and Saturdays
S Saturdays only.

OTHER TRAINS
between
New Holland and Goxhill, see Table 82

BR timetable extracts 23rd May-25th September, 1949.

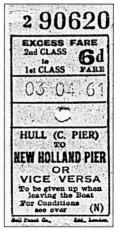

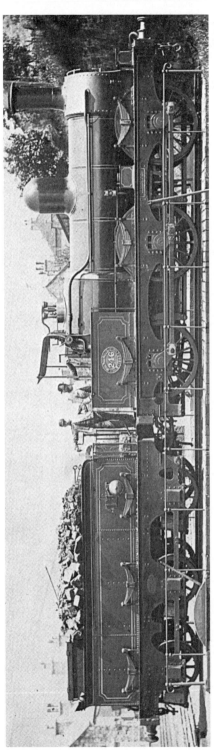

Class '23' 0-6-0 No. 246, built by Beyer, Peacock & Co. in 1862. These double-framed engines worked both goods and passenger services and were certainly regular visitors to New Holland.

Author's Collection

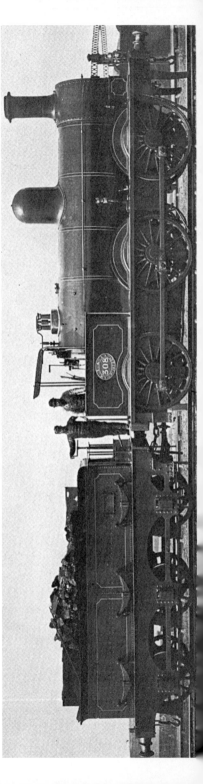

The class '18' 0-6-0 was an inside-framed contemporary of the double-framed class '23'. Built at Gorton from 1869, the class numbered 63 engines. Note the old style bent weatherboard, the crew's only protection against the elements.

Author's Collection

Chapter Five

New Holland Engine Shed and its Duties

During the period between 1847 and 1887, New Holland was regarded as the eastern terminus of the MS&L. The engine shed was built in 1847 and was provided with four roads, accessed through individual arched entrances, beneath a double pitched section roof. This was altered to two arched sections during LNER days. The shed stood alongside the southern arm of a triangle of rails formed by the Grimsby-New Holland, the Grimsby-Barton and the New Holland-Barton routes. The triangle was located to the south of New Holland Town station, its centre occupied by a reservoir, which provided water for the station and the engine shed. In the early days New Holland was dealing with traffic from all parts of the MS&LR system and from as far away as Manchester, the shed being built to deal with this kind of traffic. In 1872 New Holland was handling 45 passenger arrivals and departures, as well as 20 goods and coal trains a day.

During the 1850s the MS&L began investing heavily into the development of the port of Great Grimsby. As Grimsby grew in importance so New Holland declined. By 1887 Grimsby was the terminus of the main line from Manchester, leaving New Holland more dependent upon the fortunes of Hull.

By 1886 New Holland Shed was reduced to providing four passenger services, three of which were local; as well as goods trains to Retford, Grimsby Steetley, and Manchester. A unique survey carried out by the MS&L in the mid-1880s gives a detailed record of the entire system. It contains information about engines, crew hours worked, routes, engine miles, names of crews and even shows the amounts of oil, tallow and waste issued to each engine crew. For example, on 5th March, 1886, New Holland's workings were as follows. Engine No. 56, a 2-4-0, built in 1848, worked 16 passenger trips and two goods trains between New Holland and Barton as well as a New Holland to Cleethorpes and return, leaving New Holland at 11.30 am arriving in Cleethorpes at 12.20 pm and arriving back at New Holland at 1.42 pm. Another 2-4-0, No. 62, worked the 7.00 am from New Holland to Brocklesby, arriving at 7.50 am and returning to New Holland at 8.25 am, the engine then stood pilot between 8.30 am and 6.00 pm, when it worked an empty train to Cleethorpes. The engine worked back to New Holland with the 8.20 pm from Cleethorpes, arriving in New Holland at 9.20 pm.

Engine No. 438, a class '6B' 4-4-0, worked the 6.30 am New Holland to Manchester passenger train, arriving there at 11.20 am and departing at 2.05 pm for New Holland, where it arrived at 9.12 pm, having travelled a total of 214 miles. A second service, in the charge of engine No. 320, a 2-4-0 of 1873, left New Holland at 10. 00 am, arriving in Manchester at 12.10 pm, departing there at 4.15 pm it arrived back in New Holland at 9.12 pm.

Class '23' 0-6-0 No. 244 worked a goods train from Ardwick, departing at 12.25 am and arriving at New Holland at 8.15 am. Another class '23', No. 251, worked the 7.40 am New Holland to Retford arriving at 12 30 pm, and returning

A class '6B' 4-4-0 No. 434B built by Sacré at Gorton in December 1877. Apart from the GCR smokebox the engine is pretty well as built. A distinctive feature is the cab with its oval side window, this replaced the old weatherboard arrangement found on most rebuilt MS&LR engines until the late 1880s. The combination of outside bearings for the coupled wheels and inside for the bogie is of interest.   *Author's Collection*

An 0-6-0ST class '18T' No. 416 built at Gorton in 1880. Designed by Sacré they were known as 'Humpies' and worked as shunting engines. One such was the staple shunter for much of New Holland Shed's active life.   *Author's Collection*

An ex-NER class 'J21' 0-6-0 No. 289 stands alongside the coaling stage at New Holland Engine Shed in 1932. No. 289 and another of the same class spent nine months at New Holland Shed during this time. *N.E. Stead*

New Holland Engine Shed in June 1952 with class 'N5' No. 69305, allocated to Immingham shed, taking water. *Author's Collection*

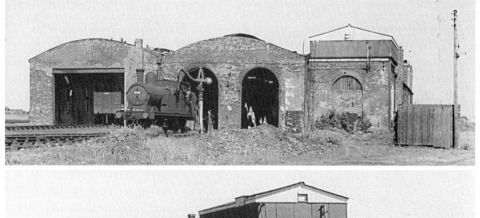

New Holland Shed looking east with the 'Yarborough Arms' in the background, photographed in July 1961. *Grimsby Public Library*

Class 'D7' 4-4-0 No. 5709 stands alongside New Holland Pier signal box with a local train, *c.* 1930. Note the weatherboard tender to protect the engine crews when working tender first in the exposed part of north Lincolnshire. No. 5709 was built in 1892 and withdrawn in March 1932. *N.E. Stead*

Ex-GNR class 'D3' 4-4-0 No. 4316 at New Holland Town station with the 1.45 pm train to Immingham Dock on 10th May, 1946. No. 4316 still sports wartime 'NE' abbreviated livery: she was scrapped in October 1949. *H.C. Casserley*

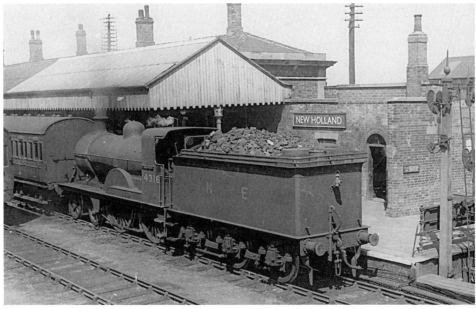

with the 1.30 pm, which arrived in New Holland at 6.45 pm. A class 'I8', 0-6-0 No. 295, worked the 11.45 am New Holland to Grimsby, arriving at 1.20 pm, the engine returned with the 3.00 pm, arriving at New Holland at 4.40 pm, where it shunted the goods yard between 6.00 and 10.00 pm.

The 1.00 pm New Holland to Retford goods was hauled by 0-6-0 No. 385; arrival in Retford was at 6.40 pm, departure at 8.30 pm and arrival back at New Holland at midnight. A further goods train, worked by a class '6A' 0-6-0, No. 396, left New Holland at 4.30 am, bound for Steetley, where it arrived at 7.50 am, returning with the 8.45 am and arriving at New Holland at 12.35 pm.

Engine No. 78 shunted at New Holland goods from 6 am to 6.00 pm, clocking up 69 engine miles, in the charge of driver F. Naylor and fireman G. Howard. Spare engines were 0-6-0s Nos. 397 and 459, 2-4-0s Nos. 33, 360 and 2-2-2 No. 58. Spare drivers were J. Franklin and J. Bell and spare firemen, J. Townsend, H. Agar and J. Robinson. Passenger crews on duty on that day were drivers T. Thompson, J. Dean, J. Richardson, C. Hill, T. Beck; and firemen G. Todd, J. Morgan, C. Malcolm, W. Dable and B. Turner. Goods crews were, drivers, N. Skelhorn, G. Franklin, J. Naylor, J. Drayton, N. Morgan; and firemen J. Parkinson, T. Rowbottom, J. Grant, J. Laverack and T. Thompson.

Things changed very little over the next few years, New Holland becoming the last outpost of the old MS&L 2-4-0s. In 1923 three class 'E' 2-4-0s still remained at New Holland and they continued for a few years under the auspices of the LNER. Also on shed in 1923 was a class 'D12', outside-framed 4-4-0. The double-framed class 'D8' 4-4-0s, relegated from express passenger work at the turn of the century, worked longer passenger runs until the arrival of the class 'D7' 4-4-0s, replaced elsewhere on the GCR sections of the LNER, at New Holland. The later class 'D9' 4-4-0s appeared during the 1930s, No. 6024 being regarded as a popular engine during its stay at the shed.

The 'D9' was used on a double shift duty, which involved trips to Retford and to Cleethorpes in the morning, and a trip to Cleethorpes and Boston, over the East Lincolnshire line of the old GNR section, in the afternoon. First duty was the 6.03 am stopping train to Retford, returning with the 8.15 am to Cleethorpes. The engine and crew returned to New Holland with the 11.15 am from Cleethorpes. At 2.15 pm the 'D9' worked a passenger train to Grimsby and from there the 3.00 pm Kings Cross passenger as far as Boston, where it arrived at 5.00 pm. It returned with a down Kings Cross departure, leaving Boston at 6.22 pm and arriving in Grimsby at 7.32 pm. This diagram operated for six years, often worked by No. 6024 crewed by either driver King and fireman Kirman, or driver Houghton and fireman Stocks.

By the time of the 1923 Grouping it became apparent that time was up for what had once been a busy shed. Immingham Shed, a few miles to the east, opened in 1912 and took over the maintenance work formerly carried out at New Holland, the latter becoming an outstation for Immingham-based engines. The LNER used mainly ex-GCR engines on its goods trains, class 'J10' and 'J12' 0-6-0s and later 'J11s'. There were usually two or three engines on shed at New Holland. Visitors were 'Sir Sam Fay', class 'B2' 4-6-0s, four-cylindered class 'B3' 4-6-0s, compound 'Atlantics' and 'Coronation' class 'A5' 4-6-2Ts usually working passenger trains operating out of Immingham or Lincoln Sheds.

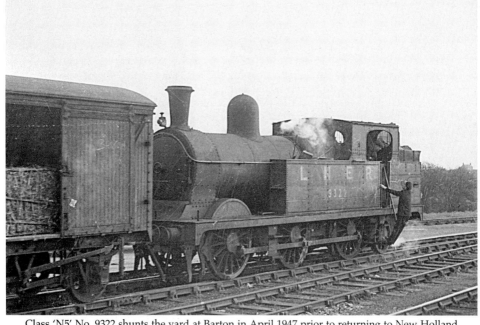

Class 'N5' No. 9322 shunts the yard at Barton in April 1947 prior to returning to New Holland with the 9.33 am passenger train.   *H.C. Casserley*

One of Robinson's magnificent 'Sir Sam Fay' class No. 1491 *City of Manchester* blasts out of New Holland Town station with the 8.30 am Pier to Cleethorpes train on 18th April, 1947.
H.C. Casserley

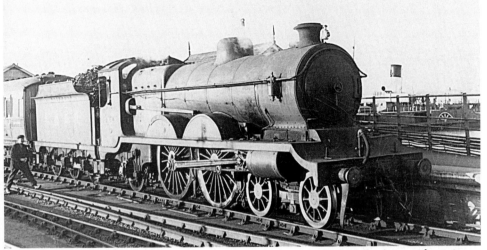

Class 'C5' Compound Atlantic, No. 2897 *Lady Faringdon* stands on New Holland pier with a train for Cleethorpes on 17th April, 1947. One of the Humber ferries is berthed alongside the pontoon.

H.C. Casserley

An immaculate looking ex-GCR class 'A5' 4-6-2 No. 69820 waits on New Holland pier with the 1.45 pm train to Immingham Dock on 28th April, 1954. No. 69820 was built in 1923 and withdrawn in November 1960, one of the last of its class to be condemned. *H.C. Casserley*

Between the mid-1930s and the 1960s, the staple shunting engine employed at New Holland was the Sentinel 'Y3'; several of these were shedded at Immingham over the years, spending much of their time at New Holland.

New Holland Shed closed officially in 1938, although it continued to function for many years afterwards. Two of the arched entrances were rather crudely knocked into one and by the 1960s the roof had gone. The only motive power in evidence was a lone diesel shunter.

As well as playing host to a variety of ancient and modern MS&L and GCR motive power, New Holland also witnessed the arrival and departure of a catholic assortment of coaching stock in some cases even more venerable than the engines; ancient MS&L coaches were still in evidence into the 1940s. A selection of stock to be found at New Holland in the 1930s, 1940s and 1950s can be found in *Appendix Two*.

Train movements around the area of the engine shed and New Holland Town and Pier stations were controlled by five signal boxes, Oxmarsh Junction, Barrow Road Crossing, New Holland Town, New Holland Pier and, at the western end of the triangle, Barton Junction. The latter disappeared a good many years ago. Although it still survives, New Holland Pier box was out of use during the latter days of operation. New Holland Town box was demolished soon after closure of the old Town station and the pier.

Class 'Y3' 0-4-0 No. 68185 shunting at New Holland on 28th April, 1954. Note the shunter's pole across the buffer beam.   *H.C. Casserley*

Chapter Six

The New Port of Immingham

In 1901 powers were obtained by the Humber Commercial Railway and Dock Company to build a new dock and other works at Immingham, together with a connecting railway. Further powers were obtained in 1904, and in that year the GCR bound itself to take a lease of the undertaking for 999 years from the completion of the works. The first sod for the new dock was cut by Lady Alexander Henderson on 12th July, 1906. The docks opened informally on 15th May, 1912, the official opening delayed in order that the King might be present. King George V opened the dock on Monday 22nd July; the cost of the project was a massive £2,599,000.

Immingham is situated on the south bank of the River Humber, nine miles east of Hull on the opposite side of the river, and six miles west of Grimsby, also on the south bank. A wide channel some 70 ft deep begins close to the entrance to the dock and continues in a straight line past Spurn Point out into the North Sea. By land the port was approached from the south by a branch five miles long off the GCR main line; from the west by a light railway (The Barton and Immingham), 6¾ miles long, which gave communication via New Holland to Hull; and from Grimsby and the east by the Grimsby and District Light Railway, seven miles in length. The speed restriction on this line was limited by the Board of Trade to 10 miles an hour. The line was acquired by the GCR who extended the west end so that it ran up to near the harbour. The line was also extended at the eastern end to run into the centre of Grimsby, the GCR employing electric traction to operate the line. The system adopted was overhead dc at 500 volts. Power was obtained from Immingham through a sub-station, where it was converted by means of two 250 kw rotary convertors, static transformers, for stepping down the current, and control panels. The rolling stock consisted of steel underframe cars carrying 64 passengers, and smaller cars carrying 40. The larger cars had two 50 hp motors and the smaller units had two 35 hp motors, giving a speed of 25 mph.

The new dock property covered 1,000 acres, was 2½ miles long and a mile wide. The river frontage extended for 1½ miles. The main dock was 1,100 ft square and the entrance lock 840 ft long by 90 ft wide. The lock gates were, at the time, the largest in the world. There were three pairs: the outer were 56 ft 6 in. high, the inner 42 ft 6 in. and the intermediate, 54 ft 6 in. The width of each leaf of gates was 53 ft 3 in. The intermediate gates served to divide the entrance into an inner lock, 520 ft long, and an outer, 320 ft in length. The depth of water was capable of dealing with any vessel afloat.

There were two arms to the dock, a south-west and a north-west, each 1,250 ft long and from 350 ft to 400 ft wide. The water area was 45 acres, or 39 if the timber pond is not included. The southern quay, opposite the entrance lock, was 2,350 ft long; the total length of quayage was 545,400 ft. Provision was made for north-east and south-east arms should these have ever been required. Parallel with the lock entrance, and to the west of it, was a graving dock, 740 ft

Guests arriving for the turning of the first sod ceremony at Immingham Docks on 12th July, 1906. Contractor's locomotive *Morecambe* is seen with some interesting stock.

Author's Collection

The ceremony of cutting the first sod of Immingham Docks, 12th July, 1906. *Author's Collection*

Although of poor quality this picture gives some idea of the scale of operation involved with the construction of Immingham Dock.

Author's Collection

GREAT CENTRAL RAILWAY.

OPENING OF

IMMINGHAM DOCK

—— BY ——

HIS MAJESTY THE KING,

MONDAY, JULY 22nd, 1912.

ADMIT *Mr W G Dempster* on board the G.C.R. S.S. "Immingham," lying in the Graving Dock.

No. 64

General Manager.

STRICTLY NON-TRANSFERABLE.

Ticket Holders are requested to be in their Seats by 1.30 p.m. at the latest.

What used to be described as 'a bird eye view' - an artist's impression of the new Immingham dock.   *Author's Collection*

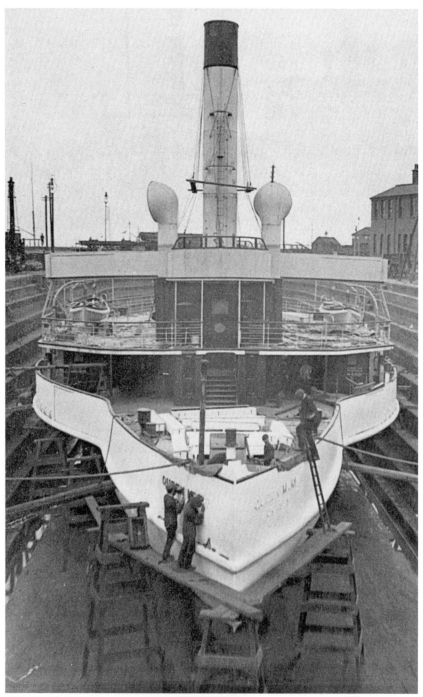

The Great Central Railway Paddle Steamer *Killingholme*, in dry dock being refurbished and renamed *Queen Mary* for the opening of Immingham Dock. She never carried the new name and carried the Royal party under her own name. *Author's Collection*

long and 56 ft wide with a water depth of 23 ft. The graving dock was divided into an inner dock, 420 ft long, and an outer, 320 ft in length, by gates of the caisson type. These, and the gates at the entrance of the graving dock were supplied by the Motherwell Bridge Company.

Leading out into the river were two jetties, one on each side of the entrance lock giving a 'V' shaped approach. These provided a large area of still water, just outside the lock entrance, saving a ship which was docking from the full force of a strong stream pressing on her quarter. The jetties were constructed of Jarrah wood and were about 650 ft long. The eastern jetty, nearer the sea, was provided with a station to deal with passenger carrying steamers. The eastern jetty was for coaling boats in the river. The largest ships were able to take on coal here, 10 miles from the open sea.

The greater part of the mineral traffic was dealt with by seven hydraulic coal hoists, 320 ft apart, on the south quay. Six of these were fixed and one, the easternmost, was movable. The latter could be employed, along with its adjoining fixed hoist, for discharging from the two holds of a boat.

Within the dock area was 170 miles of railway, including 14 reception sidings capable of holding 1,120 wagons. Into these ran trains from the collieries; if the consignments could not be dealt with immediately the wagons were placed in storage sidings, with accommodation for 8,000 vehicles. There were also 25 sidings for empty wagons, holding 2,000, as well as 14 lines on which trains were marshalled or made up. These held 1,120 wagons. Altogether there was accommodation for 100,000 tons of coal. The lines and sidings for dealing with arriving trains were separate from those handling departing trains. Immingham engine shed was built in a convenient position for both types of work, and capable of dealing with 60 locomotives.

From the reception and storage sidings the wagons were led to the high level sidings from where the coal hoists on the south quay were fed. Each hoist had eight lines from the high level, each of which held forty 10 ton or 15 ton wagons, or 320 wagons per hoist. The gradient of these lines was 1 in 100, falling towards the hoists. Each of the hoists was 100 ft high above quay level and was capable of raising 30 tons through a vertical range of 71 ft. The exception was the moveable hoist which travelled through 56 ft. The hoists could deal with end-door or bottom-delivery wagons and could handle 400 tons per hour, or 4,800 tons per 12 hour day, making a daily total for the seven hoists of 30,000 tons.

At each hoist there was a turntable for reversing any end-door wagon which arrived at the hoist with the door to the rear. After the hoist lifted the wagon the table was automatically tilted towards the dock and then back again as the hoist descended to the level of the empty wagon lines. The roads off the hoist were on a gradient of 1 in 75, falling from the dock. They passed under the high level lines by four bridges made of ferro-concrete on the Hennibique principle, to the empty wagon sidings. The six fixed hoists were supplied by Sir W.G. Armstrong, Whitworth and Company, and the moveable hoist by Messrs Tannett, Walker and Company. The hoist at the western jetty was supplied by Messrs Head, Wrightson and Company, who also built and erected the large lock gates. The jetty was connected to the mainland by a bridge about 600 ft

The PS *Killingholme* carrying the Royal party at the opening of the new dock at Immingham in 1912.   *Grimsby Public Library*

The *Dewsbury* alongside one of the coal hoists in Immingham Docks in 1912.
                                                                                                    Grimsby Public Library

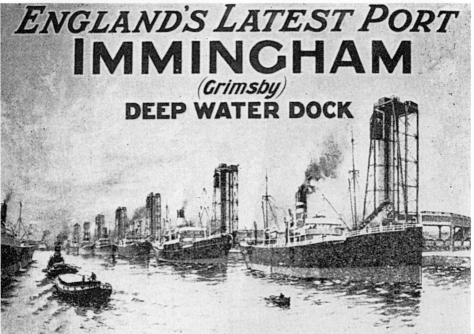

The coal hoists at Immingham; their method of operation is described in the text. *Author's Collection*

A sailing vessel being loaded with coal by the coal hoists at Immingham Dock. *Author's Collection*

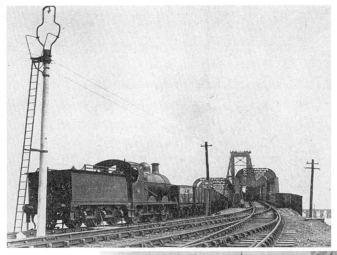

Left: GCR 0-6-0 No. 996 attends to the coal hoists at Immingham; the empty wagons are returning by gravity on the right-hand track. *Author's Collection*

Below: Passengers and luggage leaving the SS *Orford* at Eastern Jetty, Immingham and boarding the boat train. Notice the smart white coats of the train staff. *Grimsby Public Library*

An ex-GNR Ivatt class 'C1' 4-4-2 No. 1444 on a boat train special at Eastern Jetty, *c.* 1924. This traffic ceased after World War II; the jetty is now used as an oil terminal. *Grimsby Public Library*

Immingham Dock.

Reproduced from the 6", 1932 Ordnance Survey Map

long, built in six lengths of 100 ft each, the ends resting on a row of three cylinders from 9 ft to 12 ft in diameter. The cylinders had a length of 45 ft and were placed 14 ft 6 in. apart . The bridge was built in two parts, the west sides taking the full loads of the hoist, and was laid on a gradient of 1 in 90 falling towards the river. The eastern side took the empties and was laid on a 1 in 70 gradient towards the land; this hoist was capable of handling wagons of 10, 12, 15 or 20 tons capacity. The framing was of steel and consisted of triangulated legs about 84 ft in length. Special care had to be taken to obtain a foundation for these owing to the sub-structure being of timber, and they were laid on a substantial grillage of steel girders. The hoist operated and the cradle tipped by hydraulic power; the levers for controlling this were contained in the valve house, attached to the framework about 60 ft above the jetty, giving the operator a good view of the work. This hoist was capable of dealing with 43 wagons in 41 minutes. The western jetty hoist had a set of loaded wagon sidings accommodating 320 wagons and another set for a similar number of empties.

The installation of crane power was also very complete. On the north-eastern quay, to the east of the lock gates, and also on the eastern quay, there were six 2 ton double power, luffing cranes and one 10 ton crane of the same type. On the western quay, between the south-west and north-west arms, there was a 50 ton crane with a luffing jib, and on the northern wall of the south-west arm there were ten 3 ton and two 5 ton cranes. For the timber pond five 30 cwt steam travelling cranes were provided.

The hydraulic power for working the hoists, cranes, capstans etc., as well as opening and closing the lock gates, was generated in a large power house near the western jetty. There were four pairs of compound surface condensing steam pumping engines, each capable of delivering 700 gallons per minute at a pressure of 800 lb. to the square inch, and receiving their steam from nine two-flued boilers of the Lancashire type. The engines were provided with two deadweight accumulators, each having a plunger of 22 in. diameter. These automatically controlled the main engines, and were assisted in this by two other accumulators on the south side of dock, one on each side of the coal hoists. For the hydraulic service solid drawn steel pressure pipes were used.

The docks were lit by 200 electric lamps fixed on poles, the buildings illuminated by metal filament lamps, the whole represented a total candle power of about 600,000. The system was three phase ac at 6,600 volts to rotary substations, where it was converted into dc to a three wire network at 460 volts. Curtis turbo-generators were employed, situated in the same power house as the hydraulic machinery.

Three goods sheds, for handling inwards and outwards freight in transit, were built, also a granary with an elevator, automatic weighing machines, and a bonded warehouse. The general offices were situated next to the entrance lock.

In the construction of the docks over 3 million cubic yards of earthwork was excavated; this was deposited to form the yard, sidings, etc. and raised the whole site by 5 ft. Between the jetties the river was dredged and 2½ million cubic yards of material raised. This was placed in hopper barges and forced by centrifugal pumps through 12 in. pipe lines on to the land, thereby helping in

Immingham Docks marshalling yards in 1963. Rationalisation is well under way. Coal hoists Nos. 5, 6 and 7 have been dismantled, Nos. 1, 2, 3 and 4 remaining, their storage roads can be seen with the return roads positioned one between two. This was only part of the storage facilities available at Immingham. Immingham West Junction is the triangle above No. 1 coal hoist on the right of the picture, the line to the docks station curves away to the right and out of view. The Barton & Immingham line follows the coast from the junction towards the top of the view. Killingholme station was about halfway between the junction and the distant oil tanks. Here was the site of Killingholme Admiralty platform. *Grimsby Evening Telegraph*

Immingham Docks 1963. *Grimsby Evening Telegraph*

A class '6B' 4-4-0, No. 439, stands at Immingham Dock station with a train for New Holland.
E.B. Woodruffe-Peacock

Class 'D7' 4-4-0 No. 5683 stands at Immingham Dock station with a train of vintage six-wheelers on 17th March, 1934, before working an all-stations service to New Holland. *T.E. Rounthwaite*

Class 'A5' 4-6-2T No. 69820 with a train of interesting coaching stock from New Holland at Immingham Dock station (in June 1952). *Author's Collection*

The interesting station building at Immingham Dock station: the building survived long after the closure of the branch. *B. Longbone Collection*

Class 'A5' 4-6-2T No. 69820 is seen at the platform at Immingham Dock station in 1954. A new station sign has been fastened onto the original signboard. The grounded coach body and seat add a nice bit of detail. In the distance can be seen the terminus of the Grimsby-Immingham Electric Tramway. *H.C. Casserley*

Class '114' dmu No. E56028 at Immingham Dock station in the 1960s.   *R. Holden*

Immingham Shed in January 1965 with class 'B1' Nos. 61384 and 61406 and WD 2-8-0 No. 90577 'on shed'.   *Mike Black*

A view of the inside of Immingham Engine Shed in the latter days of steam with a class 'B1' 4-6-0 and Standard class '9F' 2-10-0 in evidence. *Author's Collection*

The GCR influence is still in evidence in this view of Immingham Depot, with class 'J11' No. 64284 and a class '04' 2-8-0, standing, rather forlornly near the coaling cenotaph. No. 64284 was noted in the 'New Holland Station Occurrence Book' as 'failing' at New Holland on 19th January, 1951. *N.E. Stead*

the construction. Pumping played a very important part in the execution of the works, and 39 pumps were used for various purposes. On one occasion, after a long spell of wet weather, no less than 6,700 tons of water were pumped out of the workings in the space of 16 hours.

The contractors were Messrs Price, Wills and Reeves, the consulting engineer was Sir John Wolfe Barry and the work carried out under the supervision of J.B. Ball, first as assistant engineer, but after January 1912 as chief engineer. The contractors employed as many as 2,300 men at one time. They laid 100 miles of temporary track, used 1,000 tip wagons of four yards capacity, 30 locomotives, nine steam navvies and 40 cranes from 3 tons to 10 tons capacity. In addition a 'Lubecker' steam navvy was on site, this dredged earth by a chain of buckets, similar to a marine dredger.

Despite all the latest technology employed in the construction and operation of the new port it was a very different kind of technology which caught the eye of 'Perambulator', writing in the 1920s under the title 'Heath Robinson Outdone'. At Immingham he witnessed 'something more incredibly impossible than anything Robinson himself has yet invented'.

Having enjoyed a summer weekend at Riby, near Grimsby, the writer set off with the intention of walking the 14 miles to New Holland, but found himself instead in Immingham. 'I got there quite by accident, there was no particular reason that I know of why I, or anyone else, should go there, if he could help it, or unless he were bound on one of those attractive Norwegian tours with sailings from Immingham Docks'.

The journey took our man via Habrough station. 'At Habrough the station master was pushingly enthusiastic about his trains and their convenience and reliability, and as to the amazing cheapness of the tickets he had on sale, the purchase of which would entitle me, there and then, to be carried to Hull by the 1.25 or the 3.02 with neatness and despatch. Any train, any day, one and seven return', he said. 'Perambulator' continues:

> And so to Immingham Docks, meeting railwaymen who were sure that I would not be allowed to go much further without being arrested, or, at least, turned back. And then, at last, the peace and quiet of the railway sidings, with their miles of track, and thousands of empty trucks and a sprinkling of men and boys apparently busy in keeping things in order until there is work to be done again.
>
> At last to the platform of the West Dock station itself. Having an hour to wait before my train I left the station and crossed a lock bridge to where the electric trams start for Grimsby. Hardly had I got over the water when the bridge was opened for a ship to pass, and it remained open. There was I with much less than an hour before train time, on the wrong side of the water and no sign anywhere of any intention to close the bridge again. A big notice board pointed to the refreshment room, I thought a cup of tea would comfort me in my anxiety. But the room was non-existent.
>
> Five o'clock and only twenty-five minutes to the train. Ten minutes past and only another quarter of an hour. At that moment I saw the amazing Heath Robinson contraption float slowly into view on the other side of the dock. A black barge with a high wooden causeway rigged along the top of it, and at either end a collection of ropes and pulleys and cog wheels, swinging gangways, precisely as in the magazine pictures.
>
> The barge was moored into position and made fast between the two sides of the dock, and right across the water. A magnificent naval officer of high rank - he could hardly

have been less for he had two gold stripes around each sleeve - tugged at ropes and handled bits of wire and shook refractory wheels and coaxed and lowered and raised and patted pieces of wood and lengths of boarding until there appeared from either end of the floating barge and safely on the stonework at either side of the water what was a genuine Heath Robinson bridge, for travellers like myself who had unwarily found themselves on the wrong side of Immingham dock and were in agonies of fear that they were going to miss their train and have to spend further hours taunted by a hand painted sign promising non-existent refreshments.

Over the barge I came, not daring to laugh as long as the officer stood watching me; but once safely on solid earth, with nothing between me and my train, I so shook with delight and so often turned for one last look at that marvel of pulleys and ropes, that I all but missed the train, which was full of working men who sprang from nowhere and who showed by their mere presence that there must be something going on at Immingham after all.

The terminus of the Grimsby-Immingham Electric Tramway at Immingham Docks, seen here in June 1961.   *R.M. Casserley*

Chapter Seven

The Modern Ferry Service

A letter in the *Hull Times* on 1st September, 1910, headed 'Barton-on-Humber in 2 hours 10 minutes', highlighted the conditions endured by travellers across the Humber.

I notice in your excellent paper of Tuesday 30th, a paragraph signed, 'Wet', and I can sympathise with him, as I happened to be one of the unfortunate passengers from Barton by the 9.10 pm train on Sunday night, which arrived alongside the Hull pier at 11.25 instead of 10.05, as advertised and found all trains had ceased running, and it was only right they had done as the civilised citizens of Hull do not want them running until midnight. As it was raining we had a nice treat, having to walk 3 miles to our houses and not a cab to be got. You may imagine how we felt.

How I think it is high time that the Board of Trade step in and do something for the poor unfortunate passengers that are compelled to travel with a company like the GCR, who advertise rapid luxury travel. As for the first thing, their carriages are lost in dirt, and not fit for a passenger with a decent dress to enter; and secondly, the miserable state of things you have got to put up with when you arrive at that beautiful place of change called New Holland Pier, which, in my opinion, is far more miserable to look at than Hedon Road Gaol, with waiting rooms like convicts cells, offering just a glimmering of light; and thirdly, when you board the so-called passenger steamer it is more like a farmyard than a passenger boat, dirty by being used for the conveyance of worn out horses consigned for Germany and Holland, let alone beast and sheep, and worst of all the carriers' luggage, comprising for the most part of poultry which are generally well covered with a little insect which is most troublesome to passengers.

At the same time the GCR increased their railway and steam ferry fares in the Hull and New Holland district. Political capital was made out of this by a speaker in a Unionist meeting at Barton, the assertion being that it was entirely owing to the land tax and the increased duties on licences that the company had raised its fares and that they had to do all they could to recoup and protect themselves from Government legislation. Sir Sam Fay, the General Manager of the GCR replied, 'I have to state that the adjustment of the ferry fares has nothing to do with taxation.'

The building and development of Grimsby and the new port at Immingham was looked upon with some envy by Hull. At the beginning of 1911 the Corporation were proposing to build a floating pontoon landing stage at the Victoria Pier. The Pier itself was to cost £40,000. The GCR was proposing to pay £1,500 per annum for use of the facilities. At one time the railway company contemplated running steamers from Hull to Immingham. This, however, proved impractical and it proposed instead to build six new boats, of lighter draught and faster than the existing ones, and to construct a railway direct from New Holland to Immingham as well as Grimsby. The *Hull Times* explained,

It is extremely important that the Hull Corporation should pass the poll of the people. It will so pass if the Hull people are wise and wish to increase their hold upon the trade

Right: A postcard view of Victoria Pier with the paddle steamer *Liverpool* alongside. She was an iron-built boat constructed by M. Samuelson of Hull in 1855. *Author's Collection*

Centre: A 1906 view of Victoria Pier Hull with a GCR paddle steamer alongside. *Author's Collection*

Bottom: The PS *Lincoln Castle* sporting its new British Railways' livery departs New Holland Pier for Hull. *Author's Collection*

Victoria Pier Hull

THE MODERN FERRY SERVICE 77

of the Humber. The possibilities for North Lincolnshire and its great new port at Immingham are unbounded. As touching the practical proposal of landing facilities at Hull, the argument, and it is an important one, is used, that not only is the fruit trade increasing, but there is an interesting development in the fishing trade as between Grimsby and Hull. When Grimsby is short she calls for a supply from Hull and Hull returns the compliment. Thus, by an interchange of commodity, the two ports contribute to each other's prosperity. It will be little use the GCR building improved ferry boats if they are unable to get improved facilities for discharging them. The Railway Company is itself being handicapped for want of accommodation at Hull, in much the same way as the fishing trade is being incommoded at Grimsby.

Already the Humber has a magnificent trade, but the signs of the time appear to indicate that our great waterway and the towns on its banks are only just beginning to realise the possibilities of the new future.

A GCR Report of 31st December, 1911 announced, 'Those whose business or pleasure takes them across the Humber will be pleased that two new ferry boats will be delivered to the company in a month or two.'

The first of the two new paddle steamers was launched from Earles Shipbuilding and Engineering Yard in February 1912 and named *Brocklesby*. The principal dimensions of the steamer were, length 195 ft breadth 31 ft and depth 9 ft. She was double ended, enabling her to steam equally well in either direction, and having a rudder at each end of the vessel. A spacious promenade deck with seating was provided for both 1st and 3rd class passengers.

A commodious first class saloon, with rectangular windows and large dome skylight was situated on the main deck, having a handsome entrance with an open well and double staircase, leading to a lower saloon. The saloons, as well as the smoking room, were upholstered in moquette. The windows in the first class saloon and the smoking room were fitted with inner sliding sashes containing transparent photographic views. A refreshment bar was provided.

A large cabin for 3rd class passengers, below the main deck, had rectangular port lights similar to these in the first class accommodation. The crew were berthed next to this cabin. A chart room was provided for the captain with access to the bridge. Rooms for the engineer and steward were to be found on the main deck amidships. Ample lavatory accommodation, 'of a quite superior type', was provided for passengers. Provision was made for carrying cattle, the fittings being portable. The vessels were built under the supervision of J.A. Rodger, Superintendent Engineer of the GCR, who paid particular attention to their intended service requirements.

The second paddle steamer was launched at the same shipyard and was named *Killingholme* by Mrs Boothby, wife of the assistant dockmaster at Grimsby.

During World War I the ferry boats *Killingholme*, *Brocklesby*, and *Cleethorpes* were converted into seaplane carriers. For this purpose they were equipped with derricks for lowering the planes into the sea for take off, and for retrieving them when they returned from their sortie. Their armament consisted of three small guns. The *Killingholme* was badly damaged in action and was very lucky to survive the War.

In order to continue to provide a ferry service during the War, the old

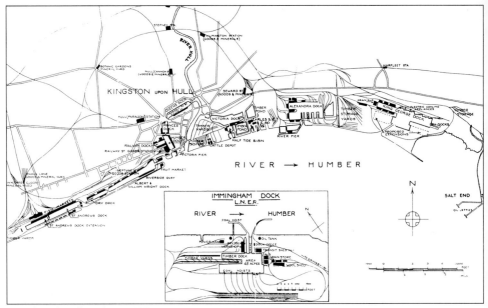

Plan of Hull Docks in 1930.

Victoria Pier, Hull with the Humber ferry alongside. Beyond is the dock basin leading to the Marina and Prince's Dock. To the right the River Hull runs into the Humber.

Author's Collection

Grimsby II, was returned to service. She was a steel built boat made by Earles, of Hull, for the MS&L in 1888. The old boat was so powerful that she made the New Holland-Hull crossing in just seven minutes. In order to maintain the 20 minute crossing schedule, her engine power was reduced, but she still took some holding. She was also used as a depot ship, providing eating and sleeping accommodation for female transport workers employed at Immingham Dock.

The old *Magna Charta II*, of 1872, was returned to service, moving cattle across the Humber and working fish traffic.

The *Mermaid* was moved up to the Humber from the south, initially to work the Goole to Hull route, but later the New Holland-Hull service. Another southern visitor was the twin-funnelled *Essex*, which, although 'sharp' at both ends to facilitate a quick turnround, proved unsuitable for the Humber.

Prior to the War the pier structure at New Holland was giving cause for concern and from 1915 a weight restriction was imposed on locomotives using the pier. It was estimated that 20 of the bays required renewing, temporary work being carried out by Logan and Hemingway at a cost of £39,240. The LNER started work on the pier in earnest in 1923, concrete stanchions replacing the wooden piers, but the new station buildings were built using recycled materials. The work took five years to complete and cost £176,463 8s. 10d.

In 1924 the *Magna Charta II* was withdrawn, after 51 years service on the Humber. Also in that year *Grimsby II* was withdrawn. She had been the first paddle steamer to be built in steel and had worked the river for 36 years.

By 1929 four vessels were working across the Humber, PS *Brocklesby*, PS *Killingholme*, PS *Cleethorpes* and PS *Frodingham*. Eighteen trips each way were made on weekdays and seven on Sundays.

Although passenger embarkation and disembarkation had steadily improved over the years, on both sides of the Humber, by the 1930s it was becoming increasingly apparent that new pontoons were required to improve the transfer of road vehicles to and from the paddle steamers. At the time the procedure for motorists wishing to avail themselves of the ferry service was to drive their vehicle onto a raft-like platform, with ropes attached to the four corners. Once the vehicle was centrally stationed it was secured to the platform, the ropes were taken up by a crane and the platform and vehicle hoisted onto the deck of the ferry. The same arrangement applied for disembarkation. This was obviously a time consuming procedure and an increasing problem as motor vehicles became more common.

It was decided that floating pontoons, 150 ft long and 50 ft wide, with connecting hinged bridges, were to be provided at both landing places. The bridges were 23 ft wide and provided with a central roadway for the use of motor vehicles, 10 ft wide and flanked by two 5 ft walkways. Both the pontoons and bridges would be covered to afford passengers some protection from the weather. At high tide the hinged bridges would be virtually level and have a maximum gradient of 1 in 9 at low tide. At New Holland the downside pontoon was completed in 1935 and the up side similarly treated after World War II. The improvements were well justified, when one considers the steady increase in motor vehicle owners willing to pay the ferry fare in order to avoid the 80 mile trip via Goole to get to either Grimsby or Hull. In 1923, 2,425

The PS *Killingholme* on the Humber ferry service backing away from the pier at New Holland.
National Railway Museum

New Holland Pier with the ferry boats *Grimsby* and *Cleethorpes* alongside the pontoon.
Grimsby Public Library

vehicles were carried, this rose steadily to 12,881 in 1938 and to 58,920 by 1955. Tonnage of merchandise during the 1920s was 102,750 and the number of cattle and sheep carried was 33,100.

Passengers were not the only beneficiaries of a regular service across the river, there was also a considerable traffic in goods in lighters hauled by tugs working between New Holland, Grimsby, Hull and Immingham. The lighters, or dumb craft, numbered 23 between the 1890s and the 1930s, with a weight capacity of 100 to 150 tons. During the 1930s forty or so trips a week were being undertaken, by the 1950s this had reduced considerably to about 25. The destination for the lighters on the north bank of the river was Hull Creek. A.W. Billany described how it was in the *LNER Magazine* of April 1947.

The name Humber Creek may conjure in your mind visions of pirates and smugglers in lonely channels and caves, but it is just that of a railway goods station occupied with traffic working, through not quite on the usual lines, we have no railway track or wagons. Our service is maintained with craft called lighters, which carry goods between Hull and New Holland.

As the distance from Hull to New Holland as the crow flies, (or the lighter sails) is just over three miles and the rail distance to New Holland via Thorne Junction is over 70 miles, one can see the advantages of a ferry service.

We are situated in an ancient and historic part of the city of Kingston-Upon-Hull, although we are in the centre of the river front, there may be many people in Hull who do not know of our existence, especially as we are now rather isolated owing to the removal of the swing bridge across the River Hull, which once gave direct access to the 'Old Town'. We are literally on an island, being separated from the city by locks, docks and the River Hull. Timber yards occupy most of the area about us, on what was known as the Citadel, where many years ago a garrison was housed.

Things are rather more peaceful now after the War, during which we were bombed and blasted, although we carried on with the exception of one occasion when we had to move on account of a heavy unexploded bomb burying itself not far from our depot.

The company (LNER) maintain a fast passenger and parcels service by paddle steamers between Corporation Pier in Hull and New Holland Pier, a journey of about 20 minutes. There is a considerable flow of traffic between New Holland and North Lincolnshire, the people of the latter area are good customers of the traders of Hull, and of course the two main fishing ports of this country, Grimsby and Hull have many things in common with a resultant good exchange of traffic.

This station, as named, cannot be found in the *RCH Handbook of Stations*. The original ferry goods station at Wellington Street was burned down in 1917. The service was transferred to the premises of the Humber Warehousing and Transport Company on the east bank of the River Hull, near where it runs into the Humber. On the demise of this firm, buildings and machinery passed into the hands of the railway company. Our traffic is collected from the town and other stations by motors and loaded into lighters by electric transporter cranes. About high-tide each day, during normal hours, the loaded lighters are taken across to New Holland by steam tug, which returns with lighters loaded at New Holland. This journey occupies about 1½ hours and when the convoy arrives here the lighters are placed in convenient berths. The contents are unloaded by the cranes and sent out for delivery or placed into warehouses.

Time and tide wait for no man and years of experience have taught us how to estimate our collections so that everything that can be possibly loaded is secured in time to catch the tide. Although we are never stopped for signal, or hot boxes, fog and rough weather can hamper our sailings, but the rivermen of the Humber are tough and it has to be a

The paddle steamer *Cleethorpes* at work on the New Holland and Hull ferry service in LNER days. This steel-built boat was constructed by Gourlay Brothers & Co. in 1903, she lasted until the mid-1930s. *E.B. Woodruffe-Peacock*

Completed by Earles Shipbuilding & Engineering Co. for the GCR in 1912, the PS *Brocklesby* survived in service until 1935/36. *E.B. Woodruffe-Peacock*

howling gale to stop them.

Traffic is loaded right up to the time of the tug's departure, there is a dash to make out invoices for the last consignment and then the documents are handed to the skipper of the 'general' up goods boat. Hatches are battened down, mooring ropes cast off, the tow rope is passed over and away glides the tug with her following.

An interesting point is that whilst the office staff, motors and drivers, checkers, loaders and cranemen are in the North Eastern Area, the lighters and crews are part of the Southern Area under the jurisdiction of the Port Master of Grimsby.

The lighter service across the Humber originated under the Steam Communications (Across the Humber) Act, 1846. This Act was repealed and re-enacted with some amendments in the MS&LR Consolidation Act of 1849. The authority to maintain the ferry service passed to the GCR and eventually to the LNER. The lighter service was not operated under specific statutory powers but was developed as an adjunct to the ferry service, by the GCR, as a means of access to Hull. The principal traffics from Hull were: wood pulp, scrap iron and steel, oil cake and grain; from Lincolnshire came iron and steel for export, basic slag for manure, sugar, oil and grain. The rates between Hull and Lincolnshire stations by lighter service were always on a lower basis than for throughout rail transit via Thorne. For this reason, and because a proportion of the traffic to and from Hull avoided certain dock charges, which would have otherwise been incurred, it was not possible for the railway company to regulate the division of traffic between the throughout and the ferry services. In order to comply with the statutory form of accounting the receipts credited to the lighter service were based on a mileage division of the throughout rate. It was necessary when assessing the financial results to consider the lighter and the rail services together. During the 1930s the lighter service consistently made a loss of between £4,207 and £5,041, although the railway's gross receipts fluctuated between £28,255 and £35,344 .

Until 1934 the railway company's tug *Barton* had dealt with towage. After that date towing was performed under contract by Foster & Company, of Hull; the company estimated a saving of about £780 per annum by contracting out.

During World War II the ferry boats again played their part in the war effort, dealing with an increased volume of traffic as well as serving as waterborne winch platforms for barrage balloons protecting the Humber ports.

The *Lincoln Castle* joined the ferry fleet in 1940. Ordered before the war, she was built by A. & J. Inglis, of Glasgow and was the last new boat to work the Humber ferry service.

Before World War II, delays were often caused to river travel by a combination of fog and low tides. On 3rd December, 1911, the *Hull Times* reported,

Wednesday was the first real foggy day of this season. All day long North Lincolnshire and the Humber was enveloped in dense fog accompanied by all the disabilities and inconveniences experienced on such days. Communication with Hull by means of the ferry service was at long intervals. People at once begin to talk about a tunnel but as soon as the fog disappears it is forgotten until the next fog arrives. Complaints about the ferry services not running are often loud and strong, but in the event of an accident

The PS *Tattershall Castle* at work on the New Holland to Hull ferry service on 10th May, 1946.
H.C. *Casserley*

The PS *Tattershall Castle* on the Humber *c*. 1954, with radar equipment in place on the bridge.
Author's Collection

The Humber ferry PS *Wingfield Castle* built by W. Gray & Co. of West Hartlepool in 1934.
Humberside Libraries

The PS *Lincoln Castle* at New Holland on 28th April, 1954. The vessel was built by A.J. Inglis Ltd, in 1940, the last new boat to be built for the service. *H.C. Casserley*

those who complain would be loud in their condemnation. It must be borne in mind that the traffic on the river, and especially steam craft, is much greater than say 20 years ago.

One of the provisions made for all stations in the New Holland area concerned the New Holland ferry during bad weather. If the ferry was made inoperative by foggy weather, passengers were not to be booked through to Hull. The system was introduced whereby New Holland would telegraph stations to Ulceby, Immingham, Barnetby and Gainsborough, each one repeating the message to a further group. The same procedure was employed when the fog cleared and the ferry service could resume.

With the advent of radar during World War II the old method of navigating the Humber, by taking soundings as the boat progressed, and listening for the bell being rung at the ferry's destination, was at once seen as antiquated. The navigational problems faced by ferry captains during fog were not so much sandbanks, tides and currents but the possibility of collision with the numerous other craft using the river, or with buoys or lightships and the like. The LNER decided to install radar on the *Tattershall Castle*, as an experiment, in 1947. However it was under the auspices of the newly formed British Railways, Eastern Region, that the equipment was installed, in January 1948 at a cost of £3,000. On 28th February, 1948, the *Hull Daily Mail* reported,

Today for the first time in its 100 years of history the Humber ferry was not delayed by the notorious Humber fog, although visibility was down to 40 yards at periods during the morning. While trawlers, which had left St Andrew's Dock, dropped anchor until it cleared, the *Tattershall Castle* steamed steadily and confidently between Hull and New Holland. This morning, for the first time, conditions on the river were bad enough to warrant its use. 'It told me everything I wanted to know' said Captain N. Waldie, after he had made two round trips. Not until he left New Holland, at 8.25 am, did conditions get really bad and visibility went down to 40 yards. But by watching the green ray sweeping over the fluorescent screen installed on the bridge, he was able to bring the ferry boat successfully through the shoals and currents of the Humber, until Victoria Pier loomed out of the mist. The Railway authorities expressed themselves highly satisfied and declared that the *Tattershall Castle* had maintained a normal service.

Eventually all ferry boats were equipped with radar, but the *Tattershall Castle* had been the first.

The *Tattershall Castle* was always regarded as the worst steamer of the last three steam ferries, the *Wingfield Castle* the best. The *Lincoln Castle* with its four, rather than three furnaces, had the greatest endurance. The three firemen, (one per shift), shovelled an average of 45 tons of coal a week as well as disposing of the burnt ash and trimming the coal. The furnaces of the Scotch marine boiler were so arranged that one or two were at face height and the others about 18 inches above the shovelling plates. Working pressure was 200 psi, blowing off at 215 psi. Economy with triple expansion engines was good, certainly more than a match for the Humber Bridge.

Chapter Eight

New Developments

During 1967 British Railways launched an investigation into the future of the Humber ferries. Important factors considered included the wisdom of ordering a new ferry fleet to replace the, by then, ageing steamers, and also the possibility of a replacement hovercraft service. Another factor for consideration was the construction of a Humber Bridge. A marvellous example of non-statement was expounded by a railway spokesperson: 'We do not want any wrong impressions to get around about the survey. It is not being done with the intention of abandoning the service, nor is it because we are thinking of replacing the ferries with hovercraft - although this is not to say that such a service might not ultimately be put into operation'.

It was estimated that the replacement of the paddle steamers would cost in the region of £2 million, with the added risk of becoming obsolete should a Humber Bridge be built. The thinking appeared to be that the paddle boats would be capable of carrying greater loads than any hovercraft available at the time, or in the foreseeable future, and also, as motoring costs rose, more motorists would avail themselves of the quickest route across the Humber by ferry.

The idea that the ferries might be replaced by either a tunnel or a bridge was not a new one. Plans were deposited on 3rd December, 1872 for the 'Hull South and West Junction Railway'. Its aim was to alleviate the restricted rail links with the rest of the country caused by the 'inadequacies of the existing railway company - the North Eastern Railway . . . The evils of this restricted accommodation has long been felt by shipping mercantile and trading communities and have at last become intolerable'.

John Fowler, engineer to the project, estimated a tunnel of about 1¾ miles in length at a cost of £375,000. In fact the proposal was for two tunnels, 10 ft below the river bed, with dimensions of 18 ft x 15 ft 6 in., ventilation appeared to have relied on draught caused by trains passing through.

The NER opposed the scheme, but local petitioning in favour ensured the Bill passed the Commons. However, by the time the Bill was presented to the Lords the MS&L and the Lancashire and Yorkshire Railway, both of which had originally favoured the scheme, had been induced by the NER to oppose its progress. This deal was achieved by the NER offering rights hitherto refused to the two companies. Counsel for the Bill maintained, 'If authority for the Bill is not given by Parliament the whole of the community will be disappointed, and an experiment which is bound to succeed, will not have been given a chance. The result will be that the North Eastern Company will have bought by money payment to the MS&L Company, and either by money payment, or money concession to the L&Y Company, a perpetuity of the monopoly which they at present possess.'

The proposers reconsidered their decision and resolved not to proceed with the Bill.

PROPOSED HUMBER BRIDGE

Drawing of bridge which the experts have suggested should be erected over the Humber between Barton and Hessle.

A drawing of the proposed Humber Bridge which was published in the *Grimsby News* in March 1930.

New Holland Town station seen in the mid-1970s with a dmu on its way down the pier.

Lens of Sutton

New Holland Pier station with a Cleethorpes-bound dmu on 27th June, 1979.   *C.A. Allenby*

It was not until 1930 that a significant proposal was put forward, this time for a road bridge. The plans were drawn up by Sir Douglas Fox & Partners who stated, 'The engineers understand that the Railway Company do not regard as a commercial proposition worth considering the finding of the capital required for their share of the crossing and that in our opinion no case for the construction of a railway crossing can be established'.

Bearing in mind that the bridge should cross the Humber where there was to be the least disturbance to navigation, and where the approaches reached high ground, it was decided the best site was due south of Hessle, on the north bank, and on the south bank the approach would start from the Barton-New Holland road on the outskirts of Barton. It was calculated that a bridge in that position would be cheaper than one on any alternative site. The cost of the works to be carried out included costings for rail and road tunnels, as well as a road or road/rail bridge, to give some comparison of alternatives.

Railway tunnels (2 tunnels each 18 ft diameter)	£4,600,000
Road tunnels (each 27 ft diameter)	£7,200,000
Road bridge	£1,725,000
Combined bridge	£4,000,000

The length of the proposed bridge, including the approach roads was estimated to be 3¾ miles.

The proposals were put before the 1930-31 session of Parliament. There was strong opposition this time from a navigation point of view. The engineers had gone to some lengths to explain that the 900 ft centre span crossed all navigable courses used for the previous 30 years. After a hearing lasting 39 days the Commons Committee passed the Bill, which then went to the House. Unfortunately, because of the financial situation the Government withdrew its promised grant and, despite attempts to find alternative means of financing the undertaking, the Bill was withdrawn. In 1937 plans were announced for a single span bridge, but due to the situation in Europe and impending hostilities the scheme did not make progress.

It was not until March 1973 that work began on what was then the longest suspension bridge in the world, using the Barton-Hessle route, favoured by several previous schemes for both tunnels and bridges. Eight years later, on 24th June, 1981, the Humber Bridge opened for business rendering New Holland Pier station and the ferries obsolete, both closed at the same time. Steve Priestly visited New Holland three times during 1981.

The first visit was about two weeks before Easter, the weather as usual, was cold, windy and overcast. This was my last visit when everything was still intact. Approximately four totems were *in situ* at the Town station as well as a black and white seat back plate on the platform seat. The large GCR bell still hung under the Town signal box nameboard. At the Pier station the Adlake lamp, (which I now have in my collection) was on the buffer stop at the end of the line, bearing the name 'New Holland' on a copper plate. This was the first time I had visited the place since the track along the pier had been singled. The other track had been removed about halfway down the pier, the rest of the track was still *in situ* but out of use and very rusty. The signals on the pier

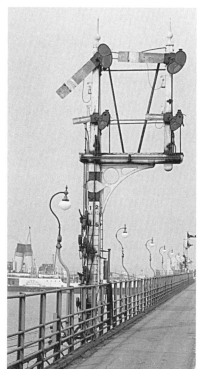

Not only a fine view of the GCR signal on New Holland pier but also the elegant lamps which illuminated both sides of the pier. Two ferries are at the pontoon in this October 1964 picture.

Author's Collection

Post-mounted shunting signals at New Holland with the balance weights immediately below the arms. The arms were for diverging lines, the top referring to the line furthest left. The numbers on the post refer to operating lever numbers.

A.A. Maclean

View looking south on 28th October, 1974 from Barrow Road level crossing. Note the interesting group of three GCR shunting signals. The up (to Ulceby) signal post carries Barrow Road signal box's starter and Oxmarsh Crossing signal box's distant. The latter's up home signal can be seen in the distance. The bracket semaphores on the down read - main post towards New Holland Town, subsidiary post (on the right-hand side) towards Barton-on-Humber. The latter stretch of line between Barrow Road and Barton Junction (controlled by New Holland signal box) was only used by the occasional freight to/from the Barton-on-Humber chemical works. Now, since the opening of the Humber Bridge, it carries the Cleethorpes-Barton-on-Humber passenger service.

C.A. Allenby

Left: The horizontally boarded standard GCR signal box at the south end of New Holland Town station on 10th June, 1973.
John Edgington

Right: The exposed New Holland Pier signal box seen here after closure.
GCRS Collection

Below: Barrow Road Crossing signal box, 6th April, 1981.
Steve Priestley

Taken on a wet day, a Barton-on-Humber train departs New Holland Pier. It will stop at New Holland Town which can just be seen in the distance, 6th March, 1980.   C.A. *Allenby*

A decidedly 'the end is nigh' look to the pier station just prior to its closing.   *Author's Collection*

had gone, all that remained were the cutdown wooden posts.

My last but one visit was on Friday 19th June, a two car dmu was in the platform at Town station and a film crew on the platform. The railcar moved over the crossing and then reversed back into the platform. The signals at the Town box did not appear to be working because the signalman gave the 'Right Away' with a green flag waved from the box. It was noticeable that all the totems had been removed, also the enamel seat back sign and several blue enamel signs. As I walked down the pier I noticed the two blue enamel signal box boards had gone (the box had been closed some years earlier). The Adlake lamp remained on the buffer stop which bore the chalked legend, 'Almost the end'. Whilst on the platform the dmu came down the pier into the station with the film crew on board, filming from the front window. I went back on the railcar to New Holland Town, first and last ride on the pier. At Town station I purchased two last day tickets for £2.50 each and an old LNER toll ticket for 3p. Several old Adlake and lamp interiors were in the station master's office; after talking to several members of staff I was given a lift, by the station master, to Barrow Road Crossing signal box. The signalman had featured in the national press, trying to buy a platform seat from New Holland Town for £25. Barrow Road box had a MS&L block instrument and GCR instruments, the wheel was of GNR vintage; apparently the car park attendant had made a bid for the instrument in Town box. I took photos in the Town box, GCR instruments, the single line tablet instrument was already removed, the tablet holders were still there, so too the lovely old clock on the wall. Whilst I was in the box the ferry arrived from Hull and the dmu left Town station.

My last visit was on Wednesday, 24th June, the Humber Bridge had opened at 11.30 am that morning. The weather was cold and windy, as usual, when I arrived at New Holland, at 5.15 pm. The car park attendant's hut was already closed, the last train had left the station at 12.15 pm, the new station, comprising a platform and bus shelter was in operation already. Both the bells had gone from the signal box, so too the signal box nameboard. The cast-iron trespass boards had been removed from Barrow Road crossing. On the platform a handful of enthusiasts were taking photos and peering through, what were now, redundant office windows. Members of staff were huddled together in a small office, marked, 'Staff Only', talking of better days and the opening of the bridge. I walked down to Barrow Road Crossing, the signalman who had wanted the platform seat, was on duty. He said that the gang had removed the instrument shelf as soon as the last train had gone through. The box was now a crossing keeper's box only.

I arrived back at the station at 5.45 and bought three old LNER tickets from the booking office for 11p. By now more people were arriving for the last ferry trip. We walked down the pier, Mr Reeves, the area manager, told us that all the relics were going to York. We went down the gangway onto the pontoon to wait for the ferry to arrive. She arrived at 6.15 pm and tied up. The boat working the last trip was the *Farringford* a diesel-electric paddle vessel, she bore a wreath on her bridge saying, 'What you leave behind no bridge can ever span'. We went on board and departed for Hull at 6.31 pm arriving at 7.14 pm. We left the ferry briefly, boarding again at 7.24 pm with a large crowd of people. Radio Humberside were on board making a live broadcast. A man on the deck played an accordion; it created quite a party atmosphere. On the return trip, the crew signed autographs, I purchased post cards and a T shirt. We arrived back at New Holland at 8.05 pm. We disembarked and waited on the pontoon for the ferry to leave for Hull. She left at 8.20 pm leaving many sad faces on the pier including Les Claxton who had been a crew member on the ferries for 34 years and was now out of a job. He said he would miss meeting people as much as anything, and had many happy memories. We shook hands, he got on his bike and rode off up the pier, not waiting for the ferry to leave. He did say that a party had been arranged on Saturday night aboard

Farringford arriving at New Holland Pier for the 6.15 pm departure, 24th June, 1981.

Steve Priestley

SEALINK UK LTD.

Final Sailings — Humber Ferry Service

Wednesday, 24th June, 1981 — Return Fare £2.50
Hull Corporation Pier — Departure 19.30 hours
New Holland Pier — Departure 18.15 and 20.00 hours

This Ticket is issued to commemorate the Last Public Sailing of the Humber Ferry Service after 150 years of crossing the Humber Estuary between Hull and New Holland

the *Farringford*.

At New Holland Town station the old clock showed 8.36 pm, all the office doors were locked and bolted. All that remained on the platform was a weather beaten board advising passengers that in adverse weather conditions the ferry would take up to 45 minutes for the crossing.

Leaving New Holland I drove to the Humber Bridge and crossed it at about 9.00 pm, the same time the ferry was to arrive at Hull for the last time. The irony was that I could not return over the bridge because a lorry had had an oil spillage and the bridge was closed. I had to return via Goole arriving home at 11.30 pm; the ferry had had the last laugh.

The pier and former New Holland Town station site have been leased to a Dutch owned bulk cargo company, called New Holland Bulk Services Ltd, who deal with the import and export of grain and other goods, including animal feeds and coal. The company laid three private sidings on the site of the old Town station with the hope of persuading British Rail to deal with their outgoing traffic; so far they have been unsuccessful and streams of lorries choke the roads. The company's 0-6-0 Rolls Royce Sentinel diesel shunter stands idle on the pier.

New Holland Dock, adjacent to the pier, has survived and its trade increased, timber, coal, steel, scrap and fertilisers being dealt with.

Many of the ex-railway staff from the area have found employment with New Holland Bulk Services, Howarth Timber or the Humber Bridge itself. Trains still run between Cleethorpes and Barton-on-Humber, with a bus connection available for Hull. The new New Holland station stands to the south of the site of its predecessor, its meagre facilities a pathetic substitute for the once splendid buildings that proclaimed New Holland the eastern terminus of the MS&L system.

New Holland Town station, 19th June, 1981.   *Steve Priestley*

The gangway at the head of New Holland Pier with the bell post. The bell used to announce the arrival of the ferry; 19th June, 1981. *Steve Priestley*

Oxmarsh Crossing signal box and gates shortly before closure in 1987. An ugly modernisation of the original box. *Andrew Ingram*

Appendix One

Locomotive Miscellany

Engine details have been compiled from the 'New Holland Station Occurrence Book', giving some idea of the locomotives working into, and around, New Holland, up until the early 1950s.

28th October, 1932	Class 'D7' 4-4-0 No. 5706 (Immingham) derailed.
14th December, 1932	Class 'J24' 0-6-0 No. 1933 (New Holland) failed.
27th February, 1933	No. 5706 failed.
20th April, 1933	Class 'D9' 4-4-0 No. 6015 (Retford) steam heating defective.
8th February, 1934	Class 'D7' 4-4-0 No. 5678 (Immingham) defective.
7th March, 1934	Class 'D7' No. 5700 (Immingham) noted.
26th March, 1934	Class 'D9' No. 5109 (Immingham) failed.
3rd May, 1935	Class 'Y3' Sentinel arrives.
5th August, 1935	Class 'K3' 2-6-0 No. 32 failed.
16th October, 1935	Class 'C1' 4-4-2 No. 9409 (New England) noted.
10th July, 1936	Class 'D7' 4-4-0 No. 5683 noted.
9th August, 1936	Class 'D2' 4-4-0 No. 4340 (Immingham) failed.
24th September, 1937	'Air Raid Precautions'.
25th November, 1938	New Holland Shed Closed.
4th April, 1939	Class 'D3' 4-4-0 No. 4316 (March) failed
13th March, 1941	Class 'D3' 4-4-0 No. 4348 (Immingham) derailed.
21st July, 1941	Class 'D9' 4-4-0 No. 6027 (Immingham) derailed.
5th June, 1943	Class 'Y3' 0-4-0 No. 94 (Immingham) failed.
23rd April, 1945	Visit of *Butler Henderson*.
25th October, 1945	No. 94 failed again.
3rd March, 1947	Class 'Y3' No. 8162 and class 'N5' 0-6-2T No. 9322 (Immingham) derailed.
28th March, 1947	Class 'Y3' No. 8179 derailed.
27th December, 1947	Class 'D3' 4-4-0 No. 2139 failed.
7th July, 1949	Class 'D2' 4-4-0 No. 4328 derailed.
27th July, 1949	Class 'D10' 4-4-0 No. 2660 (Immingham) failed.
9th August, 1949	Class 'C4' 4-4-2 No. 2919 derailed.
13th March, 1950	Class 'N5' 0-6-2T No. 9322 on the Barton service.
19th January, 1951	Class 'J11' 0-6-0 No. 64284 failed.
26th February, 1951	Class 'Y3' 0-4-0 No. 68162 noted.
8th October, 1951	Class 'Y3' 0-4-0 No. 68179 noted.
22nd October, 1951	Class 'K2' 2-6-0 No. 61724 failed at Thornton Abbey.
8th November, 1951	Class 'K2' 2-6-0 No. 61728 defective on Barton passenger.
11th March, 1953	Class 'K3' 2-6-0 No. 61827 derailed.
26th November, 1953	Class 'J11' 0-6-0 No. 64446 failed at Ulceby.

A GCR laundry van the GCR laundry was at New Holland. The vehicle was originally a mail van working between Grimsby and Tamworth via Lincoln carrying North Country mail. It was converted and re-lettered. Note the first class coupé compartment at one end.

Author's Collection

Appendix Two

Coaching Stock Miscellany

Extracted from the same source as Appendix One and demonstrating that the coaching stock at New Holland was, in some cases considerably older than some of the vintage engine stock. This situation continued until the first appearance of diesel multiple units in October 1952 which heralded the start of coach scrapping on a large scale.

27th January, 1933	No. 51057	6-wheel 3rd built Gorton 1890.
16th February, 1933	No. 51804	ex-LDEC 6-wheel 3rd built Ashburys 1897-1898.
22nd April, 1933	No. 51047	6-wheel 3rd built Gorton 1883-90.
24th June, 1933	No. 51241	6-wheel family saloon built Gorton 1896.
12th July, 1933		Train of new excursion stock arrived.
August 1933		Royal Train visited.
19th October, 1933	No. 511	ex-LDEC 6-wheel compo. 1896-7.
7th May, 1934	No. 5896	Diagram No. 124 lav. compo. 3rd Twin-Art. built Doncaster.
3rd September, 1934	No. 51019	6-wheel 1st built MS&LR 1870-89.
2nd October, 1934	No. 5130	6-wheel 3rd built Gorton 1895.
12th December, 1934	No. 51036	6-wheel 3rd built Gorton 1890.
22nd March, 1935	No. 51337	6-wheel lav. compo. built Gorton 1887-8/93-4.
5th June, 1935	No. 51263	Corridor 1st Ashburys 1898.
11th July, 1935	No. 52021	Corridor brake 3rd 1902 ECJS transferred to GC section 1925.
20th July, 1935	No. 517	6 wheel compo. MS&LR 1884.
24th October, 1935	No. 52035	1903 NER corridor 3rd ECJS transferred to GC section 1926.
30th October, 1935	No. 51824	6-wheel ex-LDEC brake 3rd built Brown Marshalls 1897.
18th August, 1936	No. 5953	6-wheel 3rd built Gorton 1888.
22nd August, 1936	No. 5830	6-wheel workman's 3rd built Gorton 1883.
31st March, 1937	No. 5863	6-wheel 3rd built Gorton 1889.
24th August, 1937	No. 5321	6-wheel workman's 3rd 1884.
29th December, 1937	No. 5385	6-wheel 3rd built Gorton 1889.
28th November, 1938	No. 5798	3rd Birmingham C&W 1905.
11th April, 1939	No. 5130	
14th July, 1939	No. 51601	6-wheel open 3rd (carriage connections) built Gorton 1899.
19th August, 1939	No. 5185	6-wheel compo. built Gorton 1877/93.
10th January, 1940	No. 51283	Corridor 3rd built Lancaster 1898.
16th March, 1940	No. 42393	Compo. Gangwayed. GNR built 1906 as No. 109.
22nd February, 1941	No. 538	3rd built GCR 1904.
19th March, 1941	No. 5457	Corridor brake 3rd built Dukenfield 1913/4 (fitted for slip detaching).
3rd July, 1952	No. 43121	Built as GNR No. 3121.
13th October, 1952		Diesel railcar trials, Lincoln District.

Appendix Three

Humber Ferry Boats

Dates Built Aqud Displ.	Name	Type	L ft	B ft	D ft	GT	NHP	Shipbuilders and Engine Builders	Machinery	Remarks	Owner
1814	Caledonia	PS								Paddle sloop. Began running on Humber 1814. Hull-Gainsborough	
1815	Humber	PS Wood								Reported working Humber traffic 1815	
1815	British Queen	PS								Reported working Humber traffic 1815	
1815	Albion	PS								Reported working Humber traffic 1815	
1815	Waterloo	PS								Reported working Humber traffic 1815	
1815	Maria	PS								Reported working Humber traffic 1815	
1831	Royal Charter	PS Wood								Working Hull-Barton Ferry 1831	
1831	Public Opinion ex Victory	PS Wood								Working Hull-Barton Ferry 1831	On hire by J. Acland from Furley & Co., Gainsborough
1832	Pelham									Hull-Grimsby	
1829	Kingston	PS Wood	76.6	17.9	9.0	60	106	Gainsborough		Working Hull-Grimsby run 1832. Sold to J. Denny 1846.	
1832*	Adelaide	PS								* Working in this year. Hull-Selby.	
1832*	John Bull	PS								* Working this year. Hull-Thorne.	
1832*	Rockingham	PS								* Working in this year. Hull-Thorne.	
1832*	Eagle	PS								* Working this year. Hull-Goole.	
1832*	Dart	PS Iron								* Working in this year. Hull-Gainsborough.	
1832*	Mercury	PS								* Working in this year. Hull-Gainsborough.	

Date	Name	Type	Length	Breadth	Depth	Tonnage	HP	Engine	Builder	Service	Notes
1832*	*Elizabeth*	PS									* Working in this year. Hull-Brigg.
1832*	*Trafalgar*	PS									* Working in this year. Hull-York.
1832* c. 1873	*Magna Charta (I)*	PS									* Working in this year. Hull-New Holland Ferry. 1848 MS&LR
1835*	*Sovereign*	PS									* Working in this year. Hull-Selby.
1841	*Ann Scarborough*	PS									Hessle-Barton Ferry
1841*	*Vivid*	PS				60					* Working in this year. Lynn-Gainsborough.
1841*	*Waterwitch*	PS									* Working in this year. Hull-London.
1843 c. 1908	*Columbine*	PS							Gainsborough		
1845*	*Falcon*	PS									* Working in this year. Hull-New Holland Ferry.
1848 1855	*Prince of Wales*	PS							Bought from Gravesend Steam Packet Co.	New Holland Ferry	1848 MS&LR
c. 1842 1848 1857	*Queen*	PS / Iron	99.25	13.8 7.5	52.4				Ditchburn & Mare, Blackwall.	New Holland Ferry	Bought second-hand from Gravesend Steam Packet Co., 1848 by MS&LR
1848 1861-78	*Manchester (I)* (Old Manchester)	PS / Iron	150	22.5	10.25			O	Robinson & Russell	New Holland Ferry	MS&LR
1848 1848 1861-78	*Sheffield (I)* (Old Sheffield)	PS / Iron							H.E. Smith, Gainsborough. J. & G. Rennie	New Holland Ferry	MS&LR
1850	*Petrel*	PS								New Holland Ferry	Hired by MS&LR from the Wartermans Co.
1851 1927	*Atlanta*	PS								Hull-Burton Stather. Hull-Ferriby. Hull-Grimsby. Excursions, etc.	Gainsborough United Steam Packet Co.
1855 1861-76	*Manchester (II)*	Iron	174			150				Hull-Burton Stather. Hull-Ferriby. Hull-Grimsby. Excursions, etc. (Formerly Clyde Steam Packet)	Bought second-hand by MS&LR in 1855 from M. Samuelson & Co. Hull
1855 1861-6	*Sheffield (II)*	PS / Iron	148			150				Hull-Burton Stather. Hull-Ferriby. Hull-Grimsby. Excursions, etc. (Formerly Clyde Steam Packet)	Bought second-hand by MS&LR in 1855 from M. Samuelson & Co. Hull
1855	*Royal Albion*	PS / Iron							Built to designs of Loco. Supt Craig	General purpose boat Humber Ferry and tug	MS&LR
1855 1855 1905	*Liverpool*	PS / Iron	159.6	18.7 8.4		220 216	80 60	1. S 2. SO, 2 cyls 2. 36"-36"	M. Samuelson, Hull. 1. M. Samuelson, Hull. 2. Laird Bros	NE. 1870; NB, 1878. New Holland Ferry	MS&LR

A wonderfully evocative photograph of possibly PS *Killingholme* crossing the Humber c. 1946. One almost gets soaked looking at it.

Peter Chapman

Dates	Name	Type	Material	L	B	D	GT	NHP	Builder	Engines	Notes	Owner
1856 / 1914	Doncaster	PS	Iron	160.5	18.7	8.4	216	80	M. Samuelson, Hull.	ditto	NE, 1875; NB, 1880 & 1892. New Holland Ferry	MS&LR
1872 / 1873 / 1924	*Magna Carta II*	PS	Iron	98.2	18.1	8.3	116	40	T. Charlton, Grimsby, ditto, Hull	LR, 1 cyl. 23½"–48"	NB, 1885. New Holland Ferry	MS&LR
1876 / 1876 / 1914	*Manchester III*	PS	Iron	159.7	18.9	8.4	221	80	Goole E. & S.B. Co. Ltd, Laird Bros	SO, 2 cycls. 36"–36"	NB, 1887. New Holland Ferry	MS&LR
1888 / 1888 / 1924	*Grimsby II*	PS	Steel	180.0	25.4	7.4	351 / 315	160 / 208	Earles S.B. & E. Co. Ltd, Hull	CDI, 2 cyls. 35", 60"–48"	New Holland Ferry	MS&LR
1890*	*Isle of Axholme*	PS									* Working on the Humber at this time. Hull-Burton Stather. Hull-Grimsby, River excursions, etc.	Gainsborough United Steam Packet Co.
1890*	*Lady Elizabeth*	PS		105	22	4					* Working in this year. Hull-South Ferriby. Excursions, etc.	Bought by Hull & Goole Steam Packet Co, 1891
1900*	*Her Majesty*	PS									* Working at this time Humber ferries.	Hull & Goole Steam Packet Co.
1900*	*Empress*	PS									* Working at this time Humber ferries.	Hull & Goole Steam Packet Co.
1903 / 1903 / 1934-6	*Cleethorpes*	PS	Steel	190.1	25.5	7.9	302	98	Gourlay Bros, Ltd.	CDI, 2 cyls. 25", 48"–45"	New Holland Ferry	GCR
1912 / 1912 / 1945	*Brocklesby*	PS	Steel	195.0	31.1	8.7	508	98	Earles Co. Ltd, Hull	CDI, 2 cyls 25", 48" 45"	New Holland Ferry	GCR
1912 / 1912 / 1945	*Killingholme*	PS	Steel	195.0	31.1	8.7	508	98	Earles Co. Ltd, Hull	CDI, 2 cyls 25", 48" 45"	New Holland Ferry	GCR
1934 / 1934	*Tattershall Castle*	PS	Steel	199.9	33.1	7.7	550	151	W. Gray & Co., W. Hartlepool Cent. Marine Eng. Wks., W. Hartlepool	TDI, 3 cycls 18", 28½",46"–51"	New Holland Ferry	LNER
1934 / 1934	*Wingfield Castle*	Steel	Steel	199.9	33.1	7.7	550	151	W. Gray & Co., W. Hartlepool Cent. Marine Eng. Wks., W. Hartlepool	TDI, 3 cycls 18", 28½",46"–51"	New Holland Ferry	LNER
1940 / 1940	*Lincoln Castle*	PS	Steel	199.7	33.1	8.8	598	120	A. & J. Inglis Ltd	TDI, 3 cycls 16½", 26", 41"–51"	New Holland Ferry	LNER

Abbreviations

L, Length; B, Beam; D, Depth; GT, Gross Tonnage; NHP, Nominal Horse Power; PS, Paddle Steamship; DI, Diagonal Engines; C, Compound Engines; T, Triple Expansion Engines; NB, New Boiler(s); LR, Lever Engines; NE, New Engines; O, Oscillating Engines; S, Simple Engines.

Note

Where two dates are given for disposal, the first indicates year in which vessel ceased to work on Humber, the second is date of scrapping. Where only one date is given with an asterisk, the vessel in question is known to have been operating in that year, dates of building and breaking up are not available.

Sources and Acknowledgements

Battle's Directory of Hull and Beverley, 1791
Battle's Directory of Hull, 1822
Hull Advertiser
Hull Corporation Archives
City Reference Library, Hull
History, Gazetteer and Directory of Lincolnshire, White, 1856
Lincoln, Rutland and Stamford Mercury
Railways and Agriculture in North Lincolnshire, Samuel Sidney, 1848
Grimsby News
Hull Daily Mail
Hull Times
Public Record Office, Kew
Illustrated London News
LNER Magazine, 1947
Great Central, (3 volumes) George Dow (Ian Allan), 1965
'Humber Ferries and the Rise of New Holland', A. Harris, *East Midland Geographer*, Vol. 15
The Humber Ferries, Alun A. D'Orley (Nidd Valley Narrow Gauge Railways Ltd), 1968
Locomotives of the LNER, Various volumes, (RCTS)
LNER Constituent Signalling, A.A. Maclean (OPC) 1983
Railways Around Grimsby, King and Hewins (Foxline) 1988
Grimsby Public Library
Great Central Railway Society

Special thanks to Bryan Longbone, Godfrey Croughton and Steve Priestley.